"*Breaking Average* is an important read for any leader who wants to elevate their team and multiply the influence and impact that they can make."

— **Mark Batterson**
New York Times Bestselling author of *The Circle Maker*
Lead Pastor of *National Community Church*

"*Breaking Average* is a skillfully-crafted, insightful resource for anyone who seeks to develop a high-performance team. Written from experience, wisdom, and a deep understanding of how leaders develop collaborative cultures, *Breaking Average* is approachable, refreshing, and empowering! It is filled with actionable tools that inspire and activate business success through team performance!"

— **Joseph Michelli**
Bestselling author of *The Airbnb Way* and *Driven to Delight*

"*Breaking Average* offers a fresh perspective on what it takes to build a team. It's a difference maker. The Seven Critical Factors alone, are invaluable. But this book goes even further. It offers relevant stories, practical tips, and a tool to help score you and your team."

— **Bonnie St. John**
Bestselling author of *Micro-Resilience*,
Paralympic Medalist and CEO, *Blue Circle Leadership*

"Interesting stories and actionable ideas will help you create a successful team or lead the team you have more effectively. Break average by reading and using this book!"

— **Mark Sanborn**
New York Times Bestselling author of *The Fred Factor*

"One of the secret weapons Amazon uses to be customer-obsessed is through how they view, build, and leverage teams (using what they call the "two-pizza rule"—no meeting can be larger than can be fed by two large pizzas). Now, in *Breaking Average*, you'll find great insight into how to build teams in any organization. The seven factors captured in this book create a framework for producing effective and productive teams to best serve your customers and clients—highly recommend."

— **Steve Anderson**
Wall Street Journal and *USA Today* Bestselling author of
The Bezos Letters

"Everyone knows that teamwork is essential to success, *Breaking Average* provides practical guidelines for building above average teams that will lead to above average results."

— **Ken Davis**
Bestselling author of *Fully Alive*,
Speaker, Communication Coach

"What does it take to build a team that will go beyond average and pursue victory until it is won? *Breaking Average* is all about how to do just that in practical ways brought to life through real life stories. Thoughtful and insightful, this book is your guide to leading others in ways that will create the extraordinary results you are looking for."

— **Chris Robinson**
Executive Vice President
Maxwell Entrepreneurial Solutions

"*Breaking Average* distills the essence of what it means and what it takes to cultivate a team. Not just any kind of team. But a team strong in leaders—leaders with the mindset and moxie to rise up to any occasion, overcome obstacles, and be victorious! This thought-provoking book provides invaluable insights to help leaders equip ordinary people to work effectively together to achieve extraordinary results."

— **Gloria Burgess**
Author, *Flawless Leadership,* and *Pass It On!*

"*Breaking Average* is a "go to" guide to help your team be successful. It offers a practical roadmap and playbook that helps leaders think strategically about improving culture and increasing teamwork."

— **Doug Taylor**
Campus Pastor, *Crossroads Church*

"After reading just the first chapter of *Breaking Average*, I couldn't wait to get the rest of the way through! I was absolutely captured by the story - who doesn't love an underdog? I love how teaching points are woven throughout!"

— **Wes Dove**
Executive Coach, *Dove Development and Consulting*

"I am adding this book to my tool bag! Not only are you led through the concept of Team Strong Leadership, but you also are introduced to a number of *Breaking Average* difference makers in their own right, who bring you immediate application discussions, tips and techniques to start implementing these factors in your life and with your team."

— **Joe Dutkiewicz**
Executive Coach, *Crayon Leadership*

BREAKING
AVERAGE

The Seven Critical Factors to
Team Strong Leadership

Paul Gustavson

with

Trudy Menke, Dave Cornell,
Mike Harbour, Barbara Gustavson,
Jay Johnson, Richard Mobley, and Gloria Burgess

Breaking Average:
The Seven Critical Factors to Team Strong Leadership
by Paul Gustavson, *et al*
Published by LEAD EDGE PRESS

Copyright © 2020 by Paul Gustavson

LEAD EDGE PRESS
c/o Discover Next Step
P.O. Box 9072
Fredericksburg, Virginia 22403

Lead Editor:	Jeff Grogan
Editorial Review:	Tiffany Johnson, and James Spann
Cover design:	Rupa Limbu
Cover image copyright:	© Adobe Stock

Published in the United States by Lead Edge Press
ISBN: 978-0-9976872-4-8

First Edition — June 1, 2020

http://breakingaveragebook.com

Table of Contents

Introduction - What Does It Take?

"What does it take to build a winning team?"

That's the question I was asked by a group of hungry entrepreneurs at a network event where I was invited to speak. They wanted my take on building a business and overcoming challenges. I was honored by the question because it's one I've asked myself.

Rather than diving straight into an answer, I responded with an inquiry of my own.

"I love that question, but why do you ask?"

All the eyes in the room darted from me to the man who asked the question. It created a split second of awkwardness that I initially regretted. Without missing a beat, the inquisitive entrepreneur responded with a profound thought.

"Well, that's the question that matters most, isn't it? You can't achieve a dream until you first build a team. So, I'm curious, what does it take?"

Heads nodded with interest. Then all eyes turned toward me.

The Question

Before I share with you what I told them. Allow me to set the table. Let me tell you why that question matters.

"What does it take?" This is the base question leaders ask when they're either in the pursuit of a goal or in the midst of a challenge. It's a universal, multi-state question that leaders ask when

they simply don't want to settle for average. It's a question of pursuit.

Not asking this question is what causes apathy. Not asking this question causes any one of us to give up and fall short of our potential. But by asking this question, we can learn to lead through any challenge or any opportunity. And leading is always about learning. It's about choosing to do something great, that takes you out of your comfort zone. It's about *breaking average.*

At the time of this writing the world is in crisis. The coronavirus is the headline news of the day. The global economy has been upended, and many businesses find themselves in the midst of a struggle. Even in the aftermath.

The challenge is real. And it's in the challenges of life that we must continue to ask the question. *What does it take?*

It's an important question because no man is an island. [1] We need each other. Never in history has it been more important to be part of a team. A team is how businesses survive – it's how we survive!

If you're like me, you want to be part of a winning team — a winning organization. None of us likes the alternative. Nobody wants to be part of a losing team — ever. Think about it. Who wants to experience a dysfunctional organization? Who wants to be part of an environment where it seems few care?

The statistics, however, are alarming. More companies and organizations, including startups and long-standing businesses, are struggling than ever before. [2] And now with the impact of a pandemic, the struggle becomes even greater. More teams are falling short and failing than we can count. If we are not careful, we will settle for average, and dysfunctionality will become the norm.

Even if the warning signs of a collapsing organization are front and center, most leaders and teams often fail to see the signs until it's too late. But it doesn't have to be this way. What this world needs — what you need — is *team strong leadership*.

Team strong leadership is defined as a team with a clear vision that draws on the insight of others through collaboration and trust. It is characterized by a sense of ownership, the courage to be resilient, and a dedication to *breaking average*. It's what leadership expert Simon Sinek might call a Just Cause, *"a specific vision of a future state that does not yet exist."* [3]

Sinek adds that this future state should be *"so appealing that people are willing to make sacrifices in order to help advance toward that vision."* Those sacrifices are part of *breaking average*.

This is the concept I ended up sharing with the entrepreneurs that day and what inspired me to write this book. And now, in the midst of a global crisis, I know this book is more important than ever.

Book Premise

The premise of this book is that any meaningful accomplishment or achievement — especially in the midst of a struggle — ultimately involves others who choose to *break average*. I can't think of a time where true success hasn't required a team.

Knowing this value of *breaking average*, I've enlisted the help of others to team with me on this topic. They know what *team strong leadership* looks like and feels like. They've graciously contributed content to support each chapter. Specifically, I've asked them for two things:

1. To share stories and lessons learned in leading successful teams that are intent on *breaking average*.
2. To offer tools and resources that will encourage leaders and empower them to make *team strong leadership* a reality no matter what the opportunity or challenge.

As a result, what you hold in your hands is more than a self-help book; it's a team playbook. It's a resource to share with anyone who wants to advance as a leader, and any individual who wants to deepen their impact as a contributor.

What's Ahead?

In this book, we explore the *breaking average* factors. When these factors are taken together, they reveal the key choices and core strengths necessary for leaders and teams. My hope is that it instills a new mindset that will create new levels of awareness, and new achievements of success – no matter what you're facing.

For this mindset to take root, it requires key behaviors to be modeled by the leader and mirrored by the team. It starts by recognizing that each team member must be seen as a contributor, for they have something to add. They are members of the team, and valuable to the cause. When we see them as contributors, they see themselves as significant.

The combination of *team strong leaders* and *team strong contributors*, who are empowered and focused by a common set of beliefs and behaviors, can unite any group or any organization. It can change the game.

However, to better understand this concept, what we need is a picture of what *breaking average* looks like. We need to begin with an example of what is possible when a team chooses to pursue their full potential despite the daunting challenges.

Chapter 1 - Working Together

"Coming together is the beginning.
Keeping together is progress.
Working together is success."
— Henry Ford

Picture yourself traveling back in time to the 1936 Olympic games. The destination is the Langer See, which is a lake just outside of the city of Berlin, Germany, near the town of Grünau.

It's just three years before World War II, and the world is already keeping a watchful eye on Hitler's Third Reich. Hitler and his war machine have designed the Olympic Games to be a propaganda platform for building nationalist pride and flexing their military moxie to the world. Their athletes are merely pawns to showcase their extremist values and cast their radical vision. Hitler wants one thing — to conquer the world.

On this unusually cold August day, there are over 75,000 people on the shore and in the grandstands on both sides of this long but narrow lake. We are anxiously awaiting the final race: the 2,000-meter rowing competition known as the Men's Eight. It's one of the biggest events of these games.

In this era, rowing is a premier Olympic sports draw. It's as big, if not bigger than track and field. For the last race today, six teams prepare to row to the starting line and represent their country. You're there to support one in particular —Team USA.

The largely German crowd is roaring with anticipation. Adding to the mayhem is a celebrity entourage in the mix that has added to the euphoria and excitement.

You peer over your shoulder into the stands. You catch the image of Adolf Hitler, the leader of the Third Reich. He's leaning on the rail, squinting through a pair of binoculars toward the dock where his German team is preparing to set their boat in the water.

As you take notice of Hitler and his entourage, you see that he is proud — almost giddy. This makes sense. Up to this point, the Germans have done well in the rowing events. In fact, the German National band has already played the Nazi party anthem a nauseating five times that day. The only respite was when the British team won gold in the 6th race: the men's double scull. It was the first time the band played something refreshingly different, UK's national anthem, *God Save The Queen*.

"Thank goodness for the queen," you hear a man next to you quietly mutter. As you turn to laugh, you recognize that the gentleman standing next to you is Al Ulbrickson, the coach of the U.S. Men's 8 crew that's about to race. [4] Ulbrickson is a square chinned, mild-mannered leader whose steel eyes soon disappear behind a pair of binoculars as he studies his team.

With one race to go, Ulbrickson knows that the host country is anticipating one last victory. The Germans are favored to win. However, Ulbrickson clearly has hopes for another team — Team USA.

This eight-man team — nine when you count the coxswain, the steersman of the boat — are all from The University of Washington, where Ulbrickson coaches. He's mentored them since they arrived as scrawny freshmen a few years earlier. Now they represent not only their school, but also their country. They are the new generation rising from the ashes of the great depression. Nobody expected them to be here.

The Journey

From the start, Coach Ulbrickson's passion was simple — to build *team strong leaders* that discovered how to work together despite the challenges.

Their improbable Olympic run started years earlier, even before their enrollment at the University of Washington. Many of them faced difficult circumstances. None of them came from homes of prominence. They worked odd and end jobs to pay for their books, meals and rent. Nothing had been given to them.

At the start of the collegiate season, well before the Olympic run, Ulbrickson was leaning toward a different boat and a different varsity crew. These 8 oarsmen and their coxswain had been relegated to the second boat.

During training, however, Ulbrickson sensed the potential that these young men had. They were scrappy, hardworking, and hungry. But he also knew they might settle for average if they didn't have the right motivation. He had relegated them to second boat as a test.

Ulbrickson wanted them to learn a simple lesson, *"If you want something bad enough, you'll find a way. If you don't, you'll find an excuse."*

Sure enough, rather than finding an excuse, they resolved themselves to find a way. In fact, they devised a plan and came up with a mantra for themselves: *"Let's Get Better."* Immediately, they went to work.

Ditching Average

Once Ulbrickson saw their commitment, he offered them another lesson: *"It's not how you start; it's how you finish."*

With that thought in mind, the team devised a *breaking average* strategy that would serve them all season long. Specifically, the tactic was to initially maintain a stroke rate slightly lower than everyone else in the first half of each race, and then take control in the home stretch.

This was not an average technique. The pattern for most teams would be to get out in front, gain momentum, and win from the start. However, for his team to win, Ulbrickson knew they couldn't think *average*. His words to them were unforgettable. *"Keep the stroke down and then mow 'em down in the finishing sprints."* [5]

It was a risky move, but he believed that they could store up enough energy to overtake their competition. When other teams would get tired, Ulbrickson's team would grow stronger. The key was for them to believe this too. Belief is a precondition for success.

Ulbrickson's next lesson was critical. *"Your beliefs alone won't make you better. Your behavior does."* Inspired, the Husky crew set out to prove their beliefs to be true. It's as if Ulbrickson knew that without belief, there could be no behavior.

The critics, however, wondered. Each race, they looked like they were always lagging behind. To the untrained eye, they looked like they weren't properly prepared. Reporters and fans questioned Ulbrickson's leadership.

The goal of a *team strong leader* is to stay true to their values. Ulbrickson's value was to finish stronger than when you start. To achieve this value, he wanted them to conserve energy and have more for the finish. It was a risky, uncommon tactic. The temptation and common practice is to always start strong. Most teams that start slow quickly lose hope. They give up when they see that they're behind. That's the risk.

Leaders like Ulbrickson transfer their beliefs to others. Belief always starts with the leader. If the leader doesn't believe, then the team won't believe. As their UW coach, Ulbrickson asked them to trust not in their eyes but in their hearts. That if they found themselves behind, they could always find a way to win.

Because of their unorthodox approach, their strategy required perfect timing. So, at the right moment in a race, the eight oarsmen would wait for the signal from the coxswain — Bobby Moch. He was the leader in the boat. He was the pacesetter, and he knew how to be patient. That's because *team strong leaders* understand the value of timing.

At the precise moment, perhaps when all seemed lost to those watching, Moch would call on his lead oarsman, Don Hume, to increase the stroke rate. Following their lead man, the rest of the team would mirror his pace.

All eight paddles synced up as they would pull their sixty-foot boat shell, the *Husky Clipper*, faster and faster through the water. Each time, their boat would close the gap and gather the momentum they needed to catch up and pull away from their competitors. Every race, all season long, their strategy worked almost flawlessly.

The Defining Moment

The University of Washington underdogs liked being in a position of knowing who was in front of them at the beginning of a race. Like a fish on a line, there was nothing more motivating to them than the feeling of reeling a big one in.

In one race, just a month before their Olympic run, it almost fell apart. It was the IRA Collegiate Regatta Championship (today we would call it the NCAA national championship). They were well behind sitting in fifth place at the midpoint. All looked lost.

Those watching that day, including Ulbrickson, begin to wonder if they were about to witness their first defeat of the season. Surprisingly though, that's when their resolve only grew stronger. That's when their belief surpassed even their coach's belief. You see on that day, his team discovered that the challenges we face are what reveal our true ability. Out of crisis comes clarity.

The 1936 Washington Husky crew found a way to come-from-behind and win. It was a defining moment for Ulbrickson as a leader — and for the crew. After the victory, it wasn't long until their mantra *"Let's Get Better"* stood for something else; *"Let's Go to Berlin."* Many believed that was Ulbrickson's idea — but it was theirs too. No one can argue that new beliefs are often spurred by the power of suggestion. It was at that moment where fans, like you, began believing this team might have a shot at Olympic glory.

Olympic Bound

After their collegiate championship, and then beating the best crew teams in the country at the U.S. Olympic Trials, the Husky crew and coach boarded the S.S. Manhattan to cross the Atlantic. This Olympic Team boat featured the likes of other athletes including Jesse Owens, Louis Zamperini, and more. They were star-struck, but they were representing their country. It was surreal.

After the long ride, these young men from Washington, seasick from their journey, stepped off the boat onto a new continent for the first time ever. It was the thing of dreams, but it almost became a nightmare.

Underdogs

Despite Team USA performing well in their preliminary races, winning each of their heats to earn a spot in the Olympic finals. It was clear they were not at their physical best. Few considered them to be a threat, and they knew it.

Unlike the other teams that made the finals, which included Germany, Italy, Hungary, Switzerland, and England, Team USA wasn't represented by a mix of their country's best oarsmen from the best colleges and professional circuit. They were still college kids. They lacked experience.

To make matters worse, Ulbrickson's lead oarsmen, Don Hume, fell sick with the flu hours before the race. He was clearly not himself, and it was affecting the rest of the team. Their confidence seemed lost. Before Ulbrickson took the stands, he addressed the team on the dock as they prepared their boat.

"Men, you earned this opportunity. You worked hard for this all season long." Then a rare smile appeared as he scanned each face. *"This is your day. You're the team nobody was ready for – all season long. The question is…"* He paused long enough to be sure he had their attention, *"are you still that team?*

"Yes Sir!" the boys responded almost in unison as they shivered in the cold.

Ulbrickson then looked directly toward Hume. *"Are you good?"*

Hume signaled he was okay and managed to offer a few words of his own despite the fatigue. *"We're still that team, coach! We want this. – I want this."* Then he glanced at his teammates, *"I won't let you down."*

Then Ulbrickson walked over to Hume and put his hand on his shoulder to address the team one last time. *"Gentlemen, we have always been the underdog. Today, is no different. But remember this. We row together, we fight together, we win together."* Then, with a rare smile Ulbrickson added, *"Just remember, keep the stroke down and then mow 'em down."*

The team laughed with nervous anticipation. It was what they needed. Ulbrickson then headed to the shoreline to find a spot to watch the race from the stands.

Moch's View

Minutes later Moch, their captain, gathered his team. The rest of them towered over him. Moch was small, light, and lacked the muscles they had, but he was their helmsman. They trusted him.

He offered one more instruction. *"Before you boys climb in that boat, I want you to see what's in front of us."* He gestured toward the lake. *"I want you to see what I see. See what's on the other side. See where we are going."*

Their eyes peered down the lake and focused on the finish line two kilometers away. The boys began to visualize. When they race, they always look backwards. They don't see the finish line until after they finally cross it, only Moch can see it from his seat as the coxswain. But today, Moch offered them a glimpse of the promised land — a view of what's to come.

Moch continued, *"At the beginning of the season, we said 'Let's Get Better'. Then it became 'Let's Go to Berlin.' Well, we're here now boys. Today, we need to finish this. Our mission is simple, 'Let's Get Busy!'*

The Race

With their boat now in the water and positioned at the starting line, Team USA ponders their circumstances.

Unfortunately, they are not in a good lane position. The German rowing team, as luck would have it, is on the far side of the river in Lane 1, closest to the trees. They are on the side that will buffer the headwinds. Germany clearly has the advantage.

Also, in a favorable lane — Lane 2 — is the Italian team. They are thought to be the best in the world by many of the critics.

Another top team, England, representing a mix of the finest British oarsmen from their country including athletes from the likes of Oxford and Cambridge, find themselves in lane 5. They are in more open waters and will likely have to deal more harshly with the headwinds than Germany or Italy.

Next to them, in lane 6, with perhaps the greatest disadvantage of all in relation to both headwinds and experience, is Team USA.

Earlier, the team was not happy with their lane position. There was no denying the odds were stacked against them, but that's how it's been all season long, and — for many — their whole life. They learned to adapt to whatever life throws their way. They are resilient.

At that moment, while waiting for the starting gun to go off, the words from their coach echo in their mind. *"We row together. We fight together. We win together."*

Ulbrickson, who is now next to you in the stands, is hopeful. He knows what his team can do. With the start of the race minutes away, Ulbrickson gazes at the team through his binoculars from his tight quarters.

As he takes stock of the team, you overhear another man nearby probe him with a question, *"Coach, how do they look? Do you think they can do it despite being in the worst lane?*

Before Ulbrickson can respond, the German fans begin a spirited chant that clearly energizes the crowd. *"Deutsch-land! Deutschland! Deutsch-land!"* You've never heard anything like it.

As the six teams position themselves before the start of the race, the crowd finally begins to quiet, and Ulbrickson turns to the man to respond to his unanswered question. *"The only lane that matters is the one they are in."* Then he adds a vote of confidence, *"They are more than ready."*

It's clear by Ulbrickson's demeanor that he believes in his team. He is proud of them. And why wouldn't he be? They have passed every test, and, despite the odds, they are ready once again. Ulbrickson appears calm, quiet, and patient. And while he's not bothered by the surroundings, truthfully, he would prefer to be unnoticed as he intently watches his team.

Meanwhile Hitler, who is present for the world to see, appears delighted yet strangely fidgety. He clearly welcomes the attention, but might he be nervous? True, he is smiling and jabbering with glee, but he acts as if they have already won. Is it a ruse? Could there be an underlying sense of insecurity? Yes, his German team is the favorite and he clearly relishes in that. Additionally, the fans have been feeding on the frenzy. They all assume that victory will be theirs. But might he be worried?

Consider for a moment these two leaders. One is Adolph Hitler perched up high in the stands with his rights and privileges. The other is Al Ulbrickson who waits in the wings in the mix of fans who were lucky enough to buy a ticket. It's clear the beliefs and behaviors between the two are vastly different. One is caught up in the hype. The other believes in the hope. One is headstrong, the other is team strong. One envisions himself as a superior leader – a ruler of the people who puts himself first. The other envisions himself as a servant leader — a believer of the people who puts his team first.

Who would you choose to lead you? The ruler or the believer? The one with the rights and privileges who is caught up in the hype? Or the one with the hunger and the humility who offers his team hope? [6]

The Start

When the starting gun finally goes off, the German team takes an immediate lead, followed by the Italian team. In the rear, as if they missed hearing the starting pistol, Team USA is barely off the line. Ulbrickson's instinct is to yell, *"Go!"* to his lagging crew, but he resists. He knows they have been there before. They're trained to keep their challenges in front of them. He trusts them.

Meanwhile in the boat, the team realizes they got a late start, but being behind is what drives them. They believe they can make up for it.

Inside the boat, Bobby Moch, the coxswain and leader, is concerned though. The late start is one thing, but the harsh wind now pushing them out of line is an added challenge. [7] At this point, most teams would be thrown off. But rather than show despair, Team USA only amplifies their urgency.

Like a quarterback calling an audible at the line of scrimmage, Moch begins barking instructions at his team as he works the rudder. Ulbrickson coached them to never quit, to never give up, and Moch is more determined than ever.

Within a few seconds Moch notices Don Hume, his lead oarsmen who sits right in front of him, is uncharacteristically slumped over. He just rows in a robotic fashion. His eyes are pinned to the floor of the boat shell. He is present but not accounted for. Moch wonders, *"Is he in a zone, or is he about to pass out? What should I do?"*

Desperate, Moch makes eye contact with Joe Rantz, who sits behind Hume as the second rower. He gestures to him to take the lead. Joe immediately understands and picks up the pace. Just then, Hume seems to awaken from his spell and begins responding to the demands of his coxswain. He feeds off the energy of his teammates behind him. They're all in sync.

Team USA's boat starts picking up the pace. They're back in the race, but they have a lot of distance to make up. Few watching believe they can close the gap. The exception is their coach, who continues to watch with laser-like intensity from his modest position in the stands.

A Fight to the Finish

Stroke after stroke Team USA begins to reel it in. They pass one boat, then two boats. But is it too late? Germany wrestles with Italy at the front of the pack. It's hard to tell who has the lead. Germany — Italy. Italy — Germany.

Except for Ulbrickson, few are watching lane 6. Despite being in the unfavorable lane, Team USA begins to inch closer to the Germans and Italians who are on the parallel side of the lake.

With just fifty meters to go, summoning all the energy they could, the American team digs even deeper. Then after six agonizing minutes of rowing, and with muscles aching for the end, three teams plow across the finish line almost simultaneously.

And the Winner Is?

It's not clear who won at first. Fans, however, are screaming. Chants of *"Deutsch-land! Deutschland! Deutsch-land!"* cascade again from both banks of the river. One member of the German crew raises his arms in victory, causing the crowd to go wild.

Meanwhile the Italians begin to celebrate as well. They believe they won!

On the opposite bank, Team USA is coasting through the water utterly spent. They have nothing left. Their muscles feel like rubber. Their chests heaved for air. As conflicting choruses of victory filled their ears, one Team USA rower managed to pant, *"Who won?"* After a long moment, another teammate responds, *"I think — I think we did!"*

A few seconds later, the PA system crackles to life and the German announcer shares the results. The fans expected to hear *"Deutschland"*. However, that was not the case. Instead the speaker announces another set of words few saw coming. *"Vereinigte Staaten von Amerika!"* — *"The United States of America!"* [8]

The hysteria and excitement from the stands halts like a sudden loss of cabin pressure. It becomes deathly quiet. The Germans were defeated, and Hitler, in frustration, is seen storming from the stands along with his posse of Nazi officials in tow. He's embarrassed.

The smattering of American fans and others who had just witnessed an amazing victory cheer the winning team as they glide back to the dock. Reluctant German fans soon begin to applaud the Americans as well. Regardless of their disappointment, no one could deny Team USA's amazing underdog win. They won by a single second. Germany came in 3rd.

At the dock, the Americans are presented with a giant, awkward winner's wreath. Then, Hitler's German National band concede their loss by playing the Star-Spangled Banner.

Can you imagine being there for that moment? Can you imagine standing in Team USA's shoes, or experiencing the win with Coach Ulbrickson?

Now visualize the same feeling in celebrating your pursuits with your team or organization. You may feel like the underdog and that the conditions are bad, but victory is more than possible, it's probable for a team that doesn't quit. Victory is the promise for those who learn to persevere. And what victory requires is *team strong leadership* centered on a desire for *breaking average.*

Seize Your Opportunities

What the 1936 U.S. Olympic rowing team accomplished represents what we all want with our team: a spirit of oneness and a feeling of victory despite the odds.

They achieved the miraculous. The same can be true for you and me. We don't need an Olympic moment to experience victory, we just need to seize the opportunities right in front of us. That's how *team strong leadership* happens.

After the big victory, the 1936 Olympic team was asked, *"How did you do it? How did you win?"* I love the responses from both the coach and the captain:

> *"Why we won can't be attributed to individuals. Every man in the boat had absolute confidence in every one of his mates."* — Al Ulbrickson (Coach)

> *"This crew was like a band of brothers — vital and valuable as the other."* — Bobby Moch (Coxswain)

Teamwork works best when we have absolute confidence in our teammates. *Team strong leadership* represents a crew of both leaders and contributors who recognize how vital and valuable they are to each other. They strive to work together and come together for the common cause of *breaking average.* [9]

Chapter 2 - Defining Teamwork

"All that I know is that
I never wanted to be average."
— Michael Jordan

We shared the story of the 1936 Olympic Rowing Team and Al Ulbrickson because it reflects so clearly the importance of *team strong leadership* and the results that we can experience when we go after *breaking average.*

Let's face it. No one wants to be average. Not Apple. Not Dell. Not Tesla Motors. Not the NFL. Not even the new church plant down the street, or the local coffee shop around the corner. So, why is it that most are simply that — average?

Why We Settle for Average

While we don't want to be average, we often settle for it. We settle for average for a number of reasons. It might be because we're too careful; we don't want to lose what we already have. We're too scared; we don't have the faith that things will be okay. Or simply we don't want to alter the status quo and risk more, so we choose to *"go along to get along."*

When we are too careful, too cautious, or too conscious of the norm, average becomes the default. Average is a low bar – that can keep being lowered. When we settle for average, it makes it an easy goal to meet — even though our intent was to aim for something higher.

Truth be told, we settle for average because we measure for average. Frankly, we don't know what else to measure. Average matters most to our control-focused minds. Average reflects the current conditions, the known metrics, and what we think are the present-day needs. [10] Average doesn't make the future better. Heck, average doesn't even help the present. Average is always about perpetuating the past, or lowering the bar — that is, until someone makes a radical disruption and *breaks average.*

The simple question to ask is this: *What if the person meant to break average and change the game is supposed to be you?* That would be pretty cool, wouldn't it? But what if you are in the midst of a crisis. Would you still go for it? Or would you settle for average?

Recognize, you don't have to do this alone. Imagine if you had a team to help you. Consider no matter how called or passionate you may be about *breaking average,* there's not much you can do without a team. That's what it takes.

Teamwork Defined

A few decades before the 1936 Olympic Games, American business mogul Andrew Carnegie presented one of the strongest definitions for teamwork that I've seen.

"Teamwork is the ability to work together toward a common vision; the ability to direct individual accomplishments toward organizational objectives. It is the fuel that allows common people to attain uncommon results."

Carnegie led the expansion of the railroad and American steel industry at the turn of the 20th century. He endured crises multiple times, and in his pursuit of *breaking average*, he experienced both success and failure. He learned what worked, and what didn't, and because of that we can learn from him.

His definition of teamwork is a result of evaluated experience. It paints a picture of what we need: a team working together to map the vision of their individual achievements to their organization's objectives.

It's been said that teamwork makes the dreamwork, but that's not entirely true. It's *breaking average* teamwork that makes the dream work. And when you don't have *team strong leadership*, then the dream can become a nightmare.

Carnegie, who was one of the most successful people of all time, started off as a very ordinary person. His first job as a telegraph messenger was for only $2.50 a week. He had to learn to be a contributor before he could become a leader. This is true of others too.

Let's explore a few additional stories of how common people attain uncommon results.

The Influence of the Other Wright

Many Americans are familiar with the legendary story of Orville and Wilbur Wright. What these bicycle shop owners crafted from a back-of-the napkin drawing and spare parts in order to launch the age of aviation is nothing short of inspirational. The effort, the grind, the persistence — all of it paid off. It changed the course of history and is the epitome of *breaking average*.

But what most people don't know is that the team it took to make this happen wasn't just Orville and Wilbur. There was another Wright — not a brother, but a sister. Katharine Wright — she was a difference maker. [11]

Years before the Wright Brothers' inaugural flight at Kitty Hawk, their father, Bishop Milton Wright, brought home a toy helicopter for his two youngest sons. The year was 1878. The toy was made of paper, bamboo, and cork, and its rotor was powered by a rubber band. Young Katharine, who was just a toddler at the time, watched her older brothers become mesmerized with the toy. They played with the helicopter for days until it broke, but their curiosity was piqued. They began to imagine one day building their own flying contraption.

Two decades later, with the encouragement of their father and younger sister, they left their bike shop in Ohio to pursue their dream of building and flying the first man-machine airplane in Kitty Hawk, North Carolina. This was a dream that others had abandoned; a dream that was thought by many to be impossible.

Despite the doubt, the Wright brothers began to experiment by flying a home-built glider off the rolling dunes of Kitty Hawk. Their adventure wasn't without challenges. Each experiment was a death-defying risk. They labored for months with no breakthroughs, only fits and slow starts. Discouraged, they almost packed it up and called it quits.

In 1901, just a year into their pursuit, Wilbur told his brother Orville that he felt defeated; that they were wasting their time and predicted that *"men would not fly for 50 years."* The comment was shared in a letter written to Katharine, who was back home in Dayton helping tend the shop. She immediately wrote back, encouraging them to continue to pursue the dream. She challenged the two to not give up and reminded them of their vision.

Encouraged by her letter, they chose to keep at it. *"Two years later,"* according to Wilbur Wright *"we ourselves were making flights."*

How did such a transformation happen? Katharine believed in the vision her brothers had and she believed that man-flight aviation was something that they could grasp. With Katharine's encouraging letter in hand, Wilbur began to believe again too.

With his vision of flight restored, he wrote back. *"It is not really necessary to look too far into the future; we see enough already to be certain that it will be magnificent."* He then spoke of his renewed urgency. *"Only let us hurry and open the roads."* Those are the thoughts of a man ready to *break average*.

When the Wright Brothers made their first controlled, man-powered flight on December 17, 1903, it changed the game. America was already shifting from an Agriculturally based nation after the Civil War to an Industrially based nation, but it was the Wright Brothers who changed the landscape entirely.

At the time of their historic flight, there were no airports. Orville and Wilbur didn't have a pilot's license. They just did it. But that's what pioneers do, and they need a team to do it.

Katharine was three years younger than her brothers, but she was the only Wright with a college education. As a teacher with a servant's heart, she practiced generosity with every act. Without their sister's relentless encouragement, the Wright Brothers may never have left the ground at Kitty Hawk. It's a reminder that it takes a team of contributors to create *team strong leadership*. It's only through *team strong contributors* that we can change the world.

Today, there are over 40,000 airports across the globe and over 130,000 commercial pilots. Of those pilots, 4,000 are female. Now, that needs to change, but do you know who the first female pilot was? You guessed it; it was Katharine Wright. In 1908, over the fields of France, Orville and Wilbur taught her how to fly the plane that she inspired them to create.

The Rise of Walt Disney

In 1934, in the wake of the Great Depression young Walt Disney, assembled a small group of animators to cast a vision for a full-length animated movie. He was only 33 years old.

His staff sat through his presentation with great curiosity — they had never seen anything like it. Disney unveiled his movie idea with a passionate performance; he acted out the entire story of *Snow White and the Seven Dwarfs*. Until that meeting, no one had ever considered making a full-length animated feature film, much less one pitched in Disney's all-in style. [12]

As animators, they had only created short films, like the classic *Steamboat Willie,* which featured Mickey Mouse. What Disney wanted to do was create a blockbuster animated film, hand-drawn, frame by frame. This would cost 10 times more than anything his studio had ever done before. Critics thought Disney was nuts, especially in the midst of economic instability, but after three years of painstaking artistry, and creative bootstrapping, he and his team found a way to get it done. The rest, as they say, is history.

Consider the impact of Disney's efforts. Based on his revolutionary film's success, *Snow White* won the Oscar for Best Musical Score and Disney himself was presented an Academy Award by the very same people who a few years earlier ridiculed him.

With the introduction of the world's first full-length animated film, Disney changed the status quo and influenced the entire American culture. His radical idea inspired a new film medium that influenced a generation of blockbusters and spawned the creation of his wildly successful theme park.

50 years after its theatrical release, the United States Library of Congress declared *Snow White* *"culturally, historically, or aesthetically significant."* [13] It is now preserved in the National Film Registry. In addition, the American Film Institute ranked Disney's movie as one of the 100 greatest American films of all time — even though it was animated. Today it is still considered the greatest American animated film ever.

What caused such a legacy of success? It was Walt Disney and his team who were focused on *breaking average*. Interestingly enough, Disney was about *breaking average* in the midst of difficult times. Consider his own bankruptcy in 1923, the Great Depression from 1928 to 1933, and World War II from 1939 to 1945. Rather than settle for average like others might have done, he chose a different path. He once said, *"Times and conditions change so rapidly that we must keep our aim constantly focused on the future."*

For Disney *breaking average* was a life pursuit – especially in the times of challenge. Why? Because he wanted to help people overcome the *"tough breaks"* which he knew were certain to come. By *breaking average*, he could change the status quo for others – maybe lift them up. And, to do that, he knew that he needed a team. It's why he said, *"It takes people to make the dream a reality."*

The Impact of Jackie Robinson

America's pastime was once an exclusively white man's sport. For decades, black players had to play elsewhere, usually in run-down facilities, and almost always to lackluster crowds. There was an unwritten segregation rule woven into the fabric of the Major League. The rule was simply this, the color of a man's skin was more important than their skill or character.

Few dared to even consider putting a man of color on their team. But that finally changed when Brooklyn Dodgers president and general manager Branch Rickey grew tired of the status quo. [14]

In 1947, Rickey signed Jackie Robinson, arguably one of the best ball players of all time. He didn't care that Robinson was black.

He cared that he was good, and a person of integrity. Although he faced intense criticism and outright abuse, Robinson changed the game forever. It started with Rickey's courage to *break average.* Was there fear? Yes. Was there doubt? You bet. Robinson himself wasn't sure about it at first. Imagined being ridiculed day after day. But they both realized the importance. They had a Just Cause.

Soon major league baseball (and many other major-league sports) became a platform to celebrate skilled players of any color and any background. Today in baseball the number #42, which is the jersey Robinson wore as a player, signifies something very special. It is a retired number that no other player can wear in the Major Leagues. It's a number that forever represents *breaking average.*

Why We Must Break Average

The point in these three stories is simply this: We must challenge average, and each of us needs a team to help make it happen.

When average is challenged, you get disruption that changes the status quo. From cultural changes like allowing women the right to vote in 1920, to allowing black baseball players in the Major League in 1947, and to innovations like the combustion engine, machine-powered flight, electric power, the personal computer, the iPhone, and electric powered cars like the Tesla Model 3. None of these disruptive ideas came easily. The pioneers of these ideas had doubters — maybe even on their own team — but they *broke average* anyhow.

Breakthroughs happen once we stop settling for average and start chasing toward doubt — not away from it. Unfortunately, our systems measure for average. Most leaders would rather play it safe than sorry. Under these conditions, our best hope is to be slightly above average — not to rock the boat, but innovative enough to make a difference. But can we?

What's really happening is most people are working to avoid being less than average. In fact, average would be celebratory. Why? Because everyone silently plays the comparison game, and the comparison game always baselines on average. Average allows us to fit in — to be accepted. It's the norm. It's the default.

At the end of the day, we don't want to lose what we already have. We want to keep the status quo, which doesn't cause problems; the status quo is to maintain average.

What if it wasn't this way? What if we set a new bar — a new metric? What if we had a new measure that didn't look back, but helped us leap ahead and break the "average" ceiling?

What it Takes

Carnegie's definition from earlier offers us insight. From his definition we learn three things about teamwork:

- It's the desire *to work together toward a common vision.*
- It's the ability *to direct individual accomplishments toward organizational objectives.*
- It's the *fuel that allows common people to attain uncommon results.*

The question we should ask is, *"What are the factors to initiate the desire, influence the ability, and ignite the fuel that leads to uncommon results?"*

This is the fundamental question of *team strong leadership*. As Carnegie suggests, there are factors like levers of influence that lead to significant breakthroughs. [15] He calls these *"uncommon results"*, which are influenced by the following elements:

- common people
- organizational objectives
- a team working together
- a personal sense of accomplishment

Carnegie's definition mentions one factor explicitly to make these *"uncommon results"* work: *"vision."* It seems that the other factors are up to us to discover.

The teamwork factors are not simply uncovered by evaluating our success. They are discovered through our struggles and lessons learned. Consider Thomas Edison, who pioneered the incandescent lightbulb, or any of the other stories I've already shared. *Overcoming average* is never based on a recipe for success, it's based on risk — and potentially failure. Facing failure and risk is how we learn, whereas success without struggle is how we stop learning.

I don't know about you, but I've learned more from my failures than my successes. Those lessons have revealed to me seven core factors that help make the dream work for any team. Each factor builds and amplifies on the other:

1. The Vision Factor
2. The Insight Factor
3. The Collaboration Factor
4. The Trust Factor
5. The Ownership Factor
6. The Resilience Factor
7. The Yes Factor

TEAMWORK FACTORS

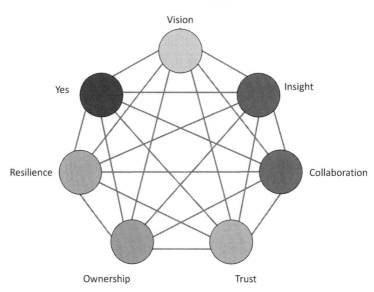

Figure 1 – Team Strong Leadership Factors

These are the core factors that every *team strong leader* should learn to recognize. While each of these factors are powerful precepts of *team strong leadership* by themselves, the sum of these factors ultimately leads a team or organization to sustainable VICTORY. Use these factors in combination to break the "average" ceiling.

The VICTORY Framework

The VICTORY Framework consists of these seven factors. Think of the factors as a seven-digit combination code needed to unlock the potential of a team and its dream. Get each factor right, and the team will discover things that satisfy their hearts' desire — relationships, rewarding experiences, and goals realized. Here's a quick look at each of the factors.

Vision

Vision is the first factor we recommend. This layer centers on the pursuit of clarity. Casting vision and gaining clarity is how you and the team can start *breaking average*!

Insight

The next part to *team strong leadership* comes through practicing insight. Insight gives us comprehension. It's important for *team strong leaders* and team members to have a hunger for comprehension.

Collaboration

While every teamwork factor is crucial, Collaboration is perhaps the most neglected. People are afraid to get out of their comfort zone and make an impact, but to collaborate well you must collide with others to garner ideas and make the team stronger. Collaboration creates team chemistry.

Trust

Trust, or the lack thereof, can make or break a team in an instant. This factor creates confidence within a team, which produces courage, which leads to more collaboration, which amplifies the team's efforts.

Ownership

In what ways are you intentional about creating a sense of ownership with your team? Ownership fosters connection amongst the members of the team, helping them build trust and search for insights to better serve that which they own.

Resilience

The Resilience Factor is ultimately about courage. When present, it allows the team to move forward despite any fear, doubt, or challenge. Any team can learn to be more resilient, and resilience complements every other *team strong leadership* factor. Without resilience, it's impossible to *break average*.

Yes

Finally, the Yes Factor is the team's commitment to the organization's vision, values, and people. When you lead and work with the Yes Factor, you embody a whatever-it-takes attitude that drives you and your team members toward growth and trust.

What's Next?

In the pages ahead, with the help of some colleagues and experts, we will explore each of these seven factors. We will highlight real-world examples of each factor and show how they can influence you and your team.

Specifically, each chapter examines the essential elements of each factor needed by 1) the leader, 2) the contributors, and 3) the overall team. This includes identifying practical tips and tools from a contributing coach's perspective to activate these essential elements. Then, we'll suggest questions that you — as a leader — can use to help build and guide your team.

Each chapter closes with a summary to further solidify the value of that specific teamwork factor.

We recommend starting with the Vision Factor; however, you can theoretically begin anywhere. Remember, each factor complements the others, no matter where you start.

Chapter 3 - The Vision Factor

FEATURING BARBARA GUSTAVSON

> *"Where there is no vision,*
> *there is no hope."*
> — *George Washington Carver*

Carnegie's definition of teamwork presented earlier identifies that a critical component to teamwork is *vision*; teamwork starts with a common vision.

That's because vision creates clarity. Think about it — a team isn't a team unless they accept a common vision. They need to know what goal they're aiming for. Clarity gives both the leader and the contributors a purpose.

Legendary NFL Hall of Fame coach Tony Dungy describes the importance of vision for a team. *"The first step toward creating an improved future is developing the ability to envision it."* And if everyone on your team can envision a similar, improved future, then a team is more likely to attain it. [16]

Vision for a New Nation

Consider the birth of the United States. It started as a vision cast by the Founding Fathers. They had a passion for their country and a vision of uniting the British colonies against an authoritarian overseas government.

The background for these legendary leaders varied. Most were lawyers, some were farmers or merchants, one was a scientist, and at least one was a land surveyor before he became an army commander and our first president. They were all sons of immigrants. They weren't born into leadership roles. They grew into them.

For the colonists who settled the land before them, America was a fresh start for the poor and persecuted. But their free and fresh start was threatened by the very nation that had sanctioned its colonization: Great Britain. [17]

Wanting more custody and control amongst the American colonists, Britain imposed new laws and taxes in Massachusetts in the mid-1770s that triggered a revolution. The colonists affectionately called these laws the Intolerable Acts.

These oppressive new laws forced Boston's key port — Boston Harbor to close until further notice. This, in addition to other Intolerable Act measures, meant many people lost their jobs, which slowed the fledgling colony's economy.

Additionally, the new laws gave British authorities immunity to any criminal prosecution, effectively placing them above the law. It created two classes of citizens: The Colonists and British government representatives.

These two classes had different rights and freedoms. For instance, it forced Colonists to open their homes to British troops without cause. They were bully tactics — a far cry from the freedom the settlers had hoped for. These Acts outraged a group of Colonist influencers and leaders — a group of men who today are known as our Founding Fathers. To the British in power however, they were merely rebel colonists.

Deep down, these colonist leaders had all grown tired of average. They called together a secret gathering in Philadelphia in 1774 in hopes of uniting the colonies to a common cause — a common vision for a new nation. Their vision would eventually be boldly identified in the Declaration of Independence.

This historical document was more than just a list of grievances, it was a declaration of a dream, a strategy, and an aspiration for the lives of all the colonists. Once this vision was set, there was no stopping these leaders from their pursuit — a pursuit that has since influenced the dreams and strategies of other nations.

The Elements of a Vision

What we can learn from our Founding Fathers and other pioneers is that vision needs three things:

1. Vision needs to be led by one or more pioneers who dare to **dream** it.
2. Vision needs to be defined and documented by a plan that others are willing to **declare**.
3. Vision needs to be pursued by a community of people willing to sacrifice to **deliver** it.

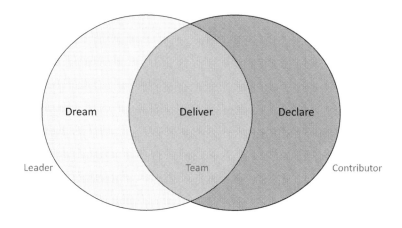

Vision

Figure 2 – The Vision Factor

Dream it, declare it, and deliver it. These elements are the three responsibilities of a vision-minded team, organization, or nation. The responsibilities require a bold leader (or leaders), a united team, and a *breaking average* strategy. These elements create the clarity needed to reach, *"uncommon results."*

In the rest of this chapter, we will explore how to cast a vision, create a strategy for the vision, and inspire others to achieve the vision using these three elements.

Dare to Dream

Though the story of the Founding Fathers seems unique, its premise is quite common, and it's also not complicated. The pattern of the Vision Factor has been modeled throughout history by others who achieved success.

Whether it marks the birth of a nation, the journey of a championship sports team, the formation of a successful company, or the creation of a relevant church, the pattern is often the same. Teamwork starts with vision that reflects the **dream** of a *team strong leader* — or set of leaders — motivated to *break average*. But aside from the examples in history, this pattern of teamwork is not as common as it could be, in part because vision has many enemies.

Vision's enemies include fear, doubt, struggle, miscommunication, mistrust, excuses, distractions, criticism, and even hyperactive logic. These enemies have thwarted the intent and progress of more potential *team strong leaders* and teams than you could possibly count.

Fortunately, these enemies can be defeated. And their demise starts by re-centering on the dream.

But what does it mean to "dream?" And why is it important to dream — especially as a leader?

A leader, as a pioneer, always carries the dream. Seldom does it come any other way. In fact, I would say a leader who does not dream cannot lead. Without a dream, you're just a manager focused on sustaining average. But true leaders and their teams — including managers — must *break average*.

To dream means to imagine not just what is, but also what could be. Dreaming allows you to think beyond your limited knowledge and activate your *team strong imagination*.

T.E Lawrence said, *"All men dream, but not equally. Those who dream by night in the dusty recesses of their minds, wake in the day to find that it was vanity: but the dreamers of the day are dangerous men, for they may act on their dreams with open eyes, to make them possible."*

As Lawrence points out, dreaming can be dangerous. Just look at the challenges great dreamers faced:

- The Founding Fathers wrote their death wish when they signed the Declaration of Independence, inviting the mighty British empire to reclaim their colonies by force.
- The Wright Brothers had little money, little support, and were almost entirely unqualified to build a man-powered plane.
- JFK's moonshot ambition was audacious, unpopular at its start and criticized as an unnecessary use of taxpayer dollars.

Every great endeavor faces resistance. True dreamers see beyond the critics, the naysayers, and their own doubts; they dream and create revolutions. One big dream can change the world, but the dream itself is not enough.

Declare the Dream

A dreamer is nothing without a team. And before the team can pursue a dream, they also need a clear vision of the goal: a **declaration**. Declarations create intent and spur action. This happens only with a tipping point, usually some sort of challenge. Among the right team, a challenge creates connection and consensus. But when the vision is too desperate or too vague, a team will often lose track of their goals and head in different directions. Then, ultimately, the dream dies.

Declaring the dream clarifies the cause. We have a term for dreams without a legitimate cause: "pipe dreams." Every great movement — every great vision — must have a cause.

In 1961, President John F. Kennedy declared a great cause. In his famous speech before Congress, he declared that we, the United States, *"should commit itself to achieving the goal, before this decade is out, of landing a man on the Moon and returning him safely to the Earth."* His moonshot goal was a bold declaration and thought by many to be impossible. But impossible is a human construct. Humans can be wrong. The only time a dream is impossible is if it's never pursued.

A leader who does not declare intent will wind up with a team that aims for different targets and chases different pursuits. But give the same team a unified vision that represents a common dream and that is presented with a clear strategy — the team will rise up to meet the challenge!

So, what is a truly declared vision? A vision's declaration doesn't just mean giving a title to a dream, it means clarifying the components of the dream. And it should also identify what the end state is. These questions help point toward the vision's declaration.

- What kind of a world do you envision?
- What current struggles or challenges might this new capability, innovation, or offering solve?
- Why is it important?

These questions lead you toward a clear declaration that a team can rally behind.

Deliver the Dream

With a dream in mind and a team behind it, there's nothing that stands in the way. You and the team can **deliver** the vision.

Consider the infamous four-minute mile. Up until 1954, no one believed a human being could run that far, that fast. It wasn't until Roger Bannister, a British college athlete studying to be a physician, was planted the vision that such a feat was possible. [18]

With his new belief and the support of his coach Franz Stampfl, Bannister took to the track and soon broke the four-minute mile in competition. Recognize the theme? Belief drives behavior.

Influenced by Bannister's example, other runners began to believe it too, and soon other athletes broke the four-minute barrier as well. In fact, only 46 days after Bannister's record mile time, an Australian named John Landy beat Bannister's. Then Bannister himself broke it again in a later competition, edging out Landy at the tape. It was the first time of many instances where multiple athletes would break the 4-minute mark in the same competition. Today, the 4-minute mile is routinely broken, and the fastest timed run for the mile today is 3:43.13.

While belief drives behavior, Bannister didn't do this alone. He needed a team. A team to train with, and a leader to guide him.

Most people think "team" is a noun. Truth be told, it's also a verb. Merriam-Webster defines the verb "team" as *"to form an association and join forces or efforts with another."* While a vision gives a reason for a team to join forces, and they must be clear on what they should do, ultimately, the team must take action; they must deliver.

Think back to JFK and the *breaking average* goal he announced in 1961. He **dreamed** it and **declared** it, but he knew America needed the best and brightest to **deliver** it as a team. [19]

The men and women who participated in the historic Mercury, Gemini, and Apollo missions devoted themselves to the moonshot ideal. Why? Because it was something bigger than themselves. It was truly a vision worth pursuing.

Team strong leadership happens when a team believes the vision is possible and unites for its success. For the moonshot vision, many people sacrificed their careers and even lives for this great pursuit. Every mistake — every tragedy — was used as momentum to further the team on the journey.

Despite tragically losing JFK, the chief visionary of the moonshot dream, in 1963, the men and women of NASA persisted in delivering his vision. Finally, on July 20, 1969, just over 8 years after President Kennedy made his bold declaration, Commander Neil Armstrong and Buzz Aldrin became the first men ever to land on the surface of the moon. The team — everyone involved, including the astronauts who came before them — helped deliver the vision. The moon landing still stands today as a country-defining, *breaking average* moment.

Gene Kranz, NASA's Apollo 11 flight director said, *"It isn't equipment that wins the battles; it is the quality and the determination of the people fighting for a cause in which they believe."* More than fifty years ago, Gene Kranz recognized the power of *team strong leadership* — and of delivering the vision.

The leader may have a strong desire to deliver the dream, but a true pioneer knows that they can't do it alone. As Helen Keller once said, *"Alone we can do so little; together we can do so much."*

A Coach's Insight

WITH BARBARA GUSTAVSON

To dig deeper, I asked my best friend and wife, Barb, who is an executive coach, to share some of her experiences related to the Vision Factor. She has personally helped me cast vision multiple times and has successfully helped others cast vision as well.

*   *   *

One of the challenges I have seen people experience is not knowing how to capture their vision. This is something I've struggled with myself at times. The good news is that there is a way to get more clarity and paint the picture they are seeking.

I remember the day clearly. I was in an intense strategy and vision retreat with my mentor Paul Martinelli, and he was helping me work through some mental roadblocks. I desperately wanted to cast my vision with clear goals.

Sensing my frustration, Paul asked me an odd question. *"Barbara, without looking around, what items in this room are blue?"* I shut my eyes and thought intently. Nothing came to mind.

Then, as if he were Mr. Miyagi, Paul asked me to walk around the room and take mental notes of every blue object.

After a few minutes, he then asked me to recall everything I saw. I identified several things perfectly. Then he asked me, *"Barbara, why didn't you notice those before?"* I thought for a moment, and realized I had seen a few of them, but just hadn't paid attention to them. He then asked me, *"what items in the room were green,"* followed shortly by the same question, but with the color yellow. In both cases, other than a few objects, I could hardly remember a thing.

It was at this point Paul once again became Mr. Miyagi. He said, *"Isn't it interesting that we only notice what we focus on, and then we miss everything else that is there all along. It's because without more awareness, we don't see a fuller picture."* That exercise with Paul taught me a valuable lesson that reminds me of John Maxwell's Law of Awareness.

We often think we need to know every detail of our vision before we can share it with our team. While it's true that the more we see, the more we can take action on, we can still choose to focus on taking action on what we *do* see, which are our values.

Our values almost always lead straight to our vision. You see, when we have clear values, we have clear vision. For whatever unknowns lie ahead, we can have faith that the other pieces of our vision will become clear as we continue to take action and trust our values.

Vision Tips for Leaders

Based on the lessons I've learned from mentors like Paul Martinelli, John Maxwell, and Doctor Daniel Amen, I've been able to create a "capture system" for my dreams and visions that has helped others too. There are multiple components to this system, but each one can lead you a step closer to a fully-fledged vision.

Tip 1 - Start with Journaling

The first tool that can help you clarify your vision is to intentionally spend time journaling and writing it out in detail. You may feel that writing is not your "thing." Let me tell you, I felt the same way until I tried it, but I have since discovered journaling to be surprisingly helpful in making decisions and creating what I want for not only my business but also other areas of my life. I recommend building journaling into your daily routine. For me, it's the most important 15-30 minutes of my morning, and it often sets the tone of my whole day.

You see, journaling isn't just about writing goals down. It's about having a conversation with yourself, as well as that wiser, deeper part of you that is often harder to hear among all the noise in your life. It's a way to expand on your deepest thoughts and answer core questions that have been eluding you. If you're still feeling unsure about how to journal, here are three simple ways to get started.

1. Review

Take a few minutes to review your goals, your strengths, and your core values. Goals identify what you want. Strengths identify what you are capable of doing. Values identify what you care about.

I keep these in the front cover of my journal. By reviewing these pillars of my personality daily, I can focus on what's important — not just for that day, but foundationally. Reviewing helps me to keep my vision front and center.

2. Reflect

Now you are ready to reflect. For this exercise, you want to simply write what comes to you drawing from your goals, strengths and values. The key is to write what comes to mind quickly — start moving your hand as soon as a thought comes to you. This helps fight our tendency to start questioning, rationalizing, and pre-editing our reflection. Rest in the knowledge that (if you write in pencil!) you can always go back and reorganize your thoughts later.

To help you reflect, think about your current or past experiences — both from an individual and team perspective — and what you can learn from them. Here are some reflective questions to help you get started:

- What am I passionate about?
- What do we care about as a team?
- How do they align?
- What do I believe is our purpose and mission?
- How am I supporting it?
- What are my strengths?

- How are my strengths being used for the team?
- What are the strengths of my teammates?
- How could they support what we want to accomplish?
- What disturbs me or rattles me?
- What is it that we want to achieve?
- How have the high points and low points of my life shaped me?
- What do I envision for the future of those we want to reach? What are their greatest needs?

Be detailed in what you write. By the end of each reflection, you should be able to identify four elements:

- Where you are (The Present)
- Where you can grow (The Potential)
- What you want to do (The Passion)
- How to get there (The Path)

Think creatively. Let your intuition take over. Be honest, open-minded, and ready for new ideas to emerge.

3. Reorient

The last step is to allow yourself a few minutes to reorient, by pulling in both the review and the reflecting part of your journal time. This helps to frame your next steps and create an even bolder vision. If you're committed to tying in your unique gifts with your vision, give yourself permission to think more boldly. Remember, boldness starts on the inside, and by reviewing, reflecting and reorienting, you are laying the groundwork to discover hidden opportunities.

Tip 2 – Capture Your *"I Have a Dream..."*

As part of your journaling practice, I also recommend taking time to capture (or recapture) your dream by using the infamous speech by Martin Luther King, Jr. as a framework.

- "I have a dream that one day this nation will rise up and live out the true meaning of its creed."
- "I have a dream that one day even the state of Mississippi, a state sweltering with the heat of injustice, sweltering with the heat of oppression, will be transformed into an oasis of freedom and justice."
- "I have a dream that my four little children will one day live in a nation where they will not be judged by the color of their skin but by the content of their character."
- "I have a dream that one day in Alabama, ... little black boys and black girls will be able to join hands with little white boys and white girls as sisters and brothers."

Notice how Dr. King incorporates all his senses. This masterful speaking technique is a perfect example of how to declare your vision to your team.

Start simply by writing your thoughts by following the statement: *"I have a dream that..."*

Tip 3 - Align Your Mindset with Your Vision

If the thoughts we believe don't align with our vision, we are going to experience resistance even if we have a solid strategy. "I am" statements are declarations of belief that can support your mindset. They are simple short messages ascribed to your character

— specifically the character you want to exhibit in sync with your vision.

Take time to capture "I am" statements that reflect who you want to be while achieving your vision. Here are a few to consider.

- I am using my gifts
- I am confident
- I am grateful
- I am happy
- I am blessed
- I am a person of action
- I am unshakable
- I am worthy of good things
- I am capable
- I am influential

When you reflect daily during your journaling time, read your "I am" statements aloud. As you tell yourself these things, they become more than just positive words. Let yourself feel them. They will help solidify your beliefs, which in turn builds your confidence and behavior.

Remember the 1936 Olympic Rowing Team? Their beliefs were a precondition for their success. And although you may be thinking that beliefs alone won't make you better, the behavior that follows always does. Behavior proves our beliefs. As a result, our beliefs, which should always be aligned with our vision, motivate our behavior, and propel both ourselves and our teams to success. That's why vision is a critical component of *team strong leadership* and the core principle of *breaking average*.

Tip 4 - Take Time to Check In

Tips 1 through 3 are more effective if the leader shares what he or she is learning with the team. Sharing your vision creates buy-in and defines the next steps. You can use the Vision Questions for Teams below to help your team engage in your vision casting. Following that, I recommend doing a leader check-in.

Check-ins between the team and the leader are an important aspect of *team strong leadership*. Here are some questions to gauge if a team is buying into your vision:

- Is the team willing and open to hear your vision? Why or why not?
- Does your team see themselves in your vision? If not, ask why, and consider adjusting the vision with your team in mind.
- Do you know what inspires each of your team members? How do each of their unique gifts play into the vision?
- How might team members' values be satisfied in the vision you've cast?
- What strengths does your team already have, and which strengths do you need to accomplish your vision?

Vision Questions for Teams

The tips we identified to cast a vision are only effective if the leader shares the vision with the team. Sharing the vision is how *team strong contributors* begin to define the necessary action steps, assign responsibilities, measure results, and adjust to changes.

The right questions allow a team to buy into both the leader and one another. Why is this important?

My mentor John Maxwell explains this well: *"People buy into the leader before they buy into the vision."* He also shares this simple but powerful formula:

Vision + Focus = Realization

Vision - Focus = Frustration

As leaders, we can help our team focus by asking them the right questions.

1. Who do you want to be?

To find the focus, team members need to first find the vision. Vision is a gift, but not everyone may be able to articulate it or appreciate it, or even understand it. One flaw is that people often start with what they want to do before they determine who they want to be. It starts by asking this question: *"What do I want to be?"*

It's okay if a team member doesn't have a crystal-clear vision yet. To get clear on your vision, get clear on your values. By knowing who they want to be, you help them identify something they value and what they want to do. Values lead to vision.

Another way to gain clarity is to ask other visions they've embraced. Did the vision of a former boss, a friend, or a trailblazing leader stir up passion in them? Think back to how John F. Kennedy mobilized the nation with his moonshot ambition, or how Martin Luther King, Jr, inspired the civil rights movement. People from vastly different backgrounds can declare and carry out a leader's vision, as long as it maps with their values.

What's not okay is settling for average with someone else's vision that doesn't align with a value. A team should always be searching for clarity.

If any member of your team is struggling to come up with a positive statement for what they want to do, you can ask them this question: *"What problem would you like to see solved?"*

Identifying a problem that should be solved reveals at least one person's values. Vision without values is like a car without an engine. You need the engine to go somewhere. The vision is where you take the car, but the values are the engine that gets you there.

2. What do you care about?

If vision is who we are on the outside and values are who we are on the inside, then we see both with our *inner eyes. Inner eyes give a team focus, and they start the engine.*

Leaders and their teams find their most important dreams with their inner eyes. This means encouraging your team to exercise a "we" mindset instead of a "me" mindset. Here are a few questions to guide your team to use their inner eyes:

- What do you care about?
- Why should we care about it?
- What can we do about it?

If they can see their own desires, they can better serve the vision because they will place their cares within the confines of the team.

3. Why does your vision matter?

Seeing is a step in the right direction, but it's not enough by itself. We can do more to further tie the leader's vision with the team's purpose. A strong purpose brings value to others. It creates connection, and here's why:

- Vision with purpose gives a team drive, making them unstoppable, even during difficult times. Think of the 1936 Olympic Rowing Team. Purpose and vision allowed them to overcome the impossible.
- Vision with purpose also acts like a GPS, giving everyone clarity on when to say "yes" and when to say "no". Think of how a GPS might give clarity on what roads to take, and which ones to avoid. With purpose and vision, decisions practically make themselves.

Here are two questions that can help you ensure your team's vision is tied to purpose.

- Why does our vision matter? (Or, What's the reason for our vision?)
- How does this vision support our purpose?

4. How do we make it a lasting vision?

If you're lucky enough to lead a team with vision, you probably know it's hard to sustain it. Periodically, check in with your team using these questions to make sure you're maintaining a long-term focus.

- Are we part of a vision/movement that could impact the world? What are the reasons we want to pursue it?
- Is our vision founded on our core values and principles? What are they?
- How might we lose our way? Are we compromising our values in any way?

5. How do we continue to create buy-in?

It's important to help others continually buy into the vision and to one another. As a leader, consider asking these questions with your team:

- What excites or inspires you about what we do?
- What are your strengths, and how do you see yourself continuing to contribute to our vision?
- What's holding us back from achieving our vision?
- What are your concerns or frustrations?
- What other opportunities do you see in front of us?

*   *   *

Key Takeaways

In this chapter, we explored why a *team strong leader* is responsible for casting a vision and engaging with the team to create buy-in. We explained that without clarity — on behalf of the leader, the contributors and the team — there can be no vision.

We learned that a clear vision consists of the following elements: a *team strong leader's* **dream**, which represents a vision, a united **declaration** by *team strong contributors,* who embrace the vision, and a unified team in pursuit of **delivering** the vision.

Former NFL Coach Tony Dungy summaries the topic of vision with this thought.

"Vision will ignite the fire of passion that fuels our commitment to do whatever it takes to achieve excellence. Vision has no boundaries and knows no limits. Our vision is what we become in life."

Dungy's words offer us powerful clarity of the Vision Factor for *team strong leaders.* Vision is where *breaking average* starts.

Chapter 4 - The Insight Factor

FEATURING RICHARD MOBLEY

"A mind when stretched by a new idea never
regains its original dimensions"
— Oliver Wendell Holmes.

After vision comes *insight*. Vision is the power to see something, whereas insight is the power to see *into* something. Don't miss the subtle difference.

Though a leader might have an authentic vision by themselves, they can't have true insight without others. Leaders need a team to garner insight. Insight creates **comprehension**. Defined, comprehension is understanding what others see and knowing what others need.

Basketball legend Michael Jordan said it well, *"Talent wins games, but teamwork and intelligence win championships."* Every team members' insight is significant. The collective insight of the team is the difference-maker between winning and losing.

Leadership author and speaker Ken Blanchard shares, *"None of us is as smart as all of us."* Insight is about the collective awareness of the team. It's not enough to simply work together — you must also understand each other's roles and goals within the team.

Team strong leaders must have a genuine interest in the thoughts and ideas of others, If there is no interest, people will find it hard to gel as a team. Insight is all about showing interest. This interest starts by expressing curiosity and being excited about what could be.

"Hidden Figures" Insight

A great example of team insight is exemplified in the movie *Hidden Figures*, which is based on the true story of a few of the amazing black female mathematicians who worked for NASA during the space race. [20] These women were instrumental in helping put a man on the moon, but, the culture being what it was in the '60s, it wasn't without some resistance.

The ability for these women to contribute and add value wasn't obvious to everyone. Fortunately, Al Harrison, a character played by actor Kevin Costner, recognized the value that others bring to the table. He was all about *breaking average.*

In one scene, he is miffed that these amazing women on his team have to walk half a mile from the building they work in because they're forced to use the colored bathroom. Fed up, he stalks across the campus and tears down the "Colored Ladies Room" sign with a crowbar. Then, he tosses the tool on the floor and says, *"There you have it. No more colored restrooms. No more white restrooms. Just plain old toilets. Go wherever you damn well please. Preferably closer to your desk. Here at NASA, we all pee the same color."*

I love that line. It's a declaration of unity reserved for a team that exemplifies insight. It's a clear example of a team that was *breaking average.*

Later in the film, Harrison needs Katherine (Goble) Johnson, a brilliant mathematician who is a black woman, to be involved in the planning required to put astronaut John Glenn into orbit around the earth. But because of NASA's rules, Johnson isn't allowed into the so-called "Go-No Go" meeting. Johnson pleads with Harrison to attend, and Harrison wants to know why.

When he asks her, "Why?", her response was both poignant and persuasive: *"Well, sir, the data changes so fast, the capsule changes, the weight and the landing zones are all changing every day. I do my work, you attend these briefings, [each time the data changes] I have to start over."*

She then adds, *"Colonel Glenn launches in a few weeks, we don't have the math figured out yet."*

Do you see the insight she offers? Insight makes the difference between an employee and a contributor; between a manager and a leader. But we've got one more step to go, because we want *team strong contributors* and *team strong leaders*.

Harrison hears every word. Harrison then wants to know from Paul Stafford, the engineer who set up the meeting, why Johnson can't attend. He initially responds that she doesn't have the proper clearance.

Katharine interrupts with fortitude. *"I feel like I'm the best person to present my calculation."*

Then Stafford responds with a comment that makes you cringe. *"And sir, she is a woman. There is no protocol for a woman to attend these meetings!"*

Harrison stiffens with his comment. *"Okay, I get that part, Stafford. But within these walls who, uh, who makes the rules?"*

Before Stafford can answer, Katherine Johnson answers for him. *"You, sir, you're the boss. You just have to act like one — sir."* Bam! Insight wins every time!

Needless to say, Harrison invites Katherine into the room. Why? Because he's not afraid of *breaking average* — and neither is she. Harrison is drawn toward *team strong contributors* and is ready to spit out the Staffords of the world who are not.

When both the leader and contributors are in pursuit of the *vision* — and have each other's *insight* — they create *team strong leadership.*

The flow of ideas is the life blood of a team. If ideas aren't flowing from team to leader and back again, how can the team engage with one another? As leadership expert John Maxwell shares, leaders, as well as contributors, need to *"be a river, not a reservoir."*

Not all ideas have to be perfect — they just need to be considered. As a leader, you should always have a few ideas to inject into the conversation, but the best leaders can coax ideas from their team through the art of great questioning. Whether it's your idea or not, the team is the best forge for *team strong insight*. Even if it's your idea, allow the team to think that it's theirs.

You can never have too many ideas. Ideas are the capital of a strong team. The team you have assembled is likely gifted with different strengths — the whole team is stronger than the sum of its parts. If you can create a space where others can engage in the pool of ideas and use their intellect, you will establish a culture of *insight*.

The Elements of Insight

Insight doesn't just happen by osmosis. Three essential elements create *insight*. First, the leader must operate with **foresight**. Second, the contributors must offer **hindsight**. And, third, the team must collectively pursue **engage-sight**. These elements are illustrated in Figure 3.

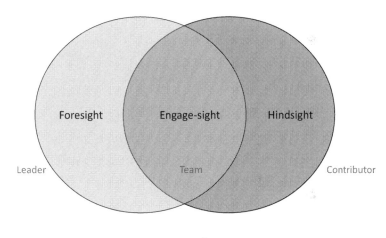

Insight

Figure 3 – The Insight Factor

Insight is all about comprehension. When all three elements of the Insight Factor are in play — foresight, hindsight, and engage-sight — there is greater comprehension for the leader, the contributors and the entire team.

These three elements, once activated, ensure that the necessary push and pull for insight is continually occurring. It's a pattern of *team strong leadership*. Think of it like the rhythm of the tides, which occur twice a day due to the moon's gravitational tug on the earth. Similarly, the Insight Factor creates a gravitational push and pull of information exchanged to and from team members. This results in greater understanding. Great teams require this rhythm of recurring insight across these three elements.

Seek Foresight

In the last chapter we talked about the Vision Factor, which is highly important to starting a team. But if you only cast a vision, you won't have *team strong leadership*. Leaders also need to *anticipate* the future; they need to have **foresight**. Foresight is intuition. It's based on what a leader knows and senses.

Specifically, foresight is a predetermination of (a) what challenges might arise, (b) how others might push back, and most importantly, (c) what benefits you and your team will enjoy when your vision comes to life.

Apple Foresight

A great example of foresight (and *breaking average*) is the formidable pair of Steve Wozniak and Steve Jobs. In 1975, Wozniak, or "Woz," as his friends called him, had the foresight to see how a microprocessor could be used with a terminal and TV monitor to create a personal desktop computer. He had more than just a vision for computers. He had a vision for the personal computer for the common man and knew instinctively what it would take; that a keyboard, screen, and computer could be integrated together into a personal package — a single box. He shares, *"This whole vision of a personal computer just popped into my head."* [21]

With foresight in mind, Woz sketched out a design that would later become the Apple I. With Wozniak's sketch and insight in hand, his partner, Steve Jobs, had the foresight to see such a computer as not just a hobbyist tool, but as the seed to grow a brand-new industry. Together, their insight was the tipping point for the personal computing era we know today. Without Jobs' and Woz's foresight, Apple, Inc. would have never been launched.

Starbucks Foresight

Another example of foresight is what Howard Shultz did for Starbucks. Under his foresight and leadership, this quaint coffee bean retailer in Seattle became a coffee service and product powerhouse that now fuels people all over the world with its signature caffeinated beverages.

Insight for Shultz happened on a trip to Milan, Italy, where he observed how a small community of people would come together at a local coffee shop that featured an exuberant barista *"doing a delicate dance as he ground coffee beans, steamed milk, pulled shots of espresso, made cappuccinos, all while chatting with customers standing side by side at the coffee bar."* [22]

Shultz observed that, *"Everyone in the tiny shop seemed to know each other, and I sensed that I was witnessing a daily ritual."* This daily ritual would inspire Schultz to chase the idea that would become the Starbucks experience you know today and would also shape the culture of coffee shops around the globe. Schultz had the foresight to see what was missing in this niche.

Share Hindsight

A leader who reflects on the steps that were taken and the impact of past decisions is one who improves in the present, not just the future. This is called **hindsight**.

Every leader has blind spots. There is something that they can't see coming. Hindsight is what mitigates the blind spots.

Hindsight centers on gathering and sharing feedback. While leaders might like to think they have hindsight on their own, the effective source of hindsight should come from everyone on the team. When a leader asks for a team member's opinion and feedback based on their evaluated experience, that team member immediately becomes a contributor.

As an analogy, think back on the 1936 American Olympic rowing team. Though there were nine people in the boat, only one of them had foresight: the coxswain. He faced toward the finish line, upriver, while his teammates pulled against the current. The coxswain was the only team member who could see where they were going, but the rest of them could see where they had been. This included seeing any teams that they had passed or were catching up. They made up for the coxswain's blind spots.

You could also say the coxswain made up for the rower's blind spots too. Remember, those rowing the boat had their back to the finish line the moment they climbed in. They could only see where they had been. They were rowing blind toward the target.

Each contributor had to trust both the coxswain to lead them and their teammates in the boat to stay in rhythm. The coxswain had the insight his rowing crew trusted, but he also needed the real-time hindsight from them to adjust and lead real-time. He would read their faces and could tell if they had more to give or if he needed to back off — or if there was another boat sneaking up on them.

You can't be in sync with your team without their hindsight. It doesn't need to wait until the after-action review. Improvement requires continuous review and simultaneous evaluation from the team. That's how you erase blind spots.

In a nutshell, hindsight happens when you have multiple perspectives of what's going right, and what could be better. When we are open to other perspectives based on experience, we often have an *"Oh, I get it now"* moment of awareness. And when a leader has a moment of awareness with their team, they develop a bond that can serve as a catalyst for *team strong leadership*.

Offer Engage-sight

The combination of foresight and hindsight opens the door for the third type of insight: **engage-sight**. Engage-sight is a quality of a culture reflected by two key behaviors. [23]

1. Be proactive in connecting with others
2. Seek to understand before being understood

Verizon Engage-sight

Many years ago, Verizon had a series of commercials that featured a technician walking from place to place, usually winding up in the middle of nowhere, checking the service's cell phone coverage. Every few steps he would hold his phone to his ear and ask, *"Can you hear me now?"*

This iconic marketing campaign depicted how hard Verizon was working to make sure their customers had superior coverage everywhere. Through almost a decade of advertising, many people were convinced by their message and network maps, which showed red dots saturating most of North America, that Verizon was the superior cell phone carrier.

The *"Can you hear me now?"* message created a first-impression moment centered on engage-sight. That's because this factor of *insight* requires engagement and empathy. In Verizon's case, the empathy was the persona of a hardworking technician as their spokesman going where you would go to find a gap in the signal. And the empathy was also to show that they had your town covered in red.

As consumers, we want our favorite brands, organizations, and teams to show an interest in us. We want to know that we, the consumers, are on their mind and matter to them most. When a leading brand recognizes that consumers both exist and are important, we reciprocate — we buy more. When we — as customers, subscribers, and fans — are first on their mind, we become even more ravenous followers. At the end of the day, this is a very human drive: we don't want to be forgotten.

This is why we prefer companies, brands, and leaders who have engage-sight. Engage-sight is engagement mixed with empathy. Without empathy, engagement becomes just a survey of consumers to see what they'll buy in order to sell more stuff. As leaders, what we can learn from this is that business shouldn't be about selling more, business should be about serving more.

Empathy puts a business in the shoes of their consumers — like what the Verizon commercial symbolized by having one of their own "walking in the shoes" of a customer.

Engage-sight is critical to both your team's success and your success. If you are a leader, engage-sight starts with you. You can't just delegate it. You need to be involved in gathering insight by showing both engagement and empathy. Your example steers your team's culture.

To create culture, you want your team to rally together and to engage with one another. Engage-sight creates collisions with others so we can stand in their shoes. In this way, it allows others to become leaders.

When engage-sight is practiced properly, it's a reminder that leadership is not about position, it's about the person with the opportunity to act. Everyone has the potential to influence others.

No matter whom you lead, there are leaders throughout your team. They may not have a leadership title, but everyone leads themselves and influences others.

From the leader to the contributor, engage-sight involves someone stepping into the role of the end user with empathy. Think back to Howard Schultz's Starbucks revelation. It didn't happen behind a desk, it happened with the leader getting away from his desk and exploring the environment he wanted to serve.

Peter Drucker, a well-respected management consultant and author, once said, *"The most important thing in communication is hearing what isn't said."* Hearing what isn't said requires empathy. People who practice engage-sight put themselves in a *team-strong* position to contribute their ideas in the pursuit of *breaking average.*

A Coach's Insight

WITH RICHARD MOBLEY

To dig deeper, I asked Richard Mobley, a good friend of mine and an executive coach, to share some of his experiences. I'm fascinated with his knack of helping others with insight, so I turned to him for guidance on this topic.

*   *   *

It's true. At the time of this writing, I have officially become a senior citizen. As with most things, there are good and bad qualities to aging. One of the good things is having a longer view of past accomplishments and failures. As I reflect, I find that having *insight* has been a key to the successes my teams and I have enjoyed, but the lack of insight has contributed to our failures.

Sometimes we confuse *insight* as vision, but vision usually refers exclusively to the future. While leaders must have vision, as we shared in the last chapter, they need something more. John Maxwell says, *"Leaders need wisdom and discernment for the present. They need to be able to look at complex situations, gain clarity, and determine a course of action."*

Foresight involves a deliberate mindset that asks, *"what if"* rather than *"yeah, but."* Foresight believes there is always at least one way forward. Have you ever had a problem, opportunity, or challenge where you just knew what to do? That's foresight at work.

Years ago, I was working for a company and courting a potential client. We exchanged several emails and voicemails and I talked numerous times with his assistant. The first time I met him face-to-face was at an industry event. When I shook hands with him and finally looked him in the eye, a thought jumped into my mind. *"This would be a great person to work with and for."* At the time, I wasn't looking for a job change. However, less than a year later, my company was sold, and guess who I ended up working for?

That was foresight at work. And in hindsight, he was the best leader I ever worked for.

Insight Tips for Leaders

Experience has taught me that the best way to accomplish the insight factor (especially engage-sight) is by listening. Listen and observe everyone with your utmost attention. People will always tell you what they're really thinking — sometimes non-verbally — if you'll only listen and observe.

Tip 1 - Observe the Needs

If you can't understand how different people see the world, you won't be able to observe them accurately. There are many

73

models to understand the spectrum of human personality, and they all work well to some degree. Personally, I have found that the DISC model has been a valuable tool to help me understand both myself and others in the workplace.

We're all factory-wired with certain traits, and while we're all a blend of each personality style, we often respond based upon the most dominant one. What we discover is that people are generally predictable.

When I want to listen better, be more empathetic, or gain a better perspective with someone different than me, I ask myself two questions from the basic DISC test:

1. Is this person more outgoing or more reserved?
2. Is this person more task-oriented or more people-oriented?

Armed with the answers to these questions, I am better equipped to engage the person in a manner that fits their needs. This is the power of engage-sight. It's not always about intuition — sometimes you need a system's help. For me, DISC helps me cut through the small talk and reach real issues. Knowing the person's DISC style helps me achieve engage-sight in the here and now.

Tip 2 - Evaluate the Experience

Have you ever heard the statement *"Experience is the best teacher?"* Well, that cliché is wrong — experience is not the best teacher. Evaluated experience is the best teacher. Experience, unless it's evaluated, doesn't buy you anything other than maybe a picture and a post for Facebook.

However, when you take the time to evaluate your experiences, you gain engage-sight — you gain knowledge. As Evan Esar said, *"There's many a forward look in a backward glance."* By looking back and learning, you and your team can know what to do going forward.

Tip 3 - Ride the Wave

A friend of mine is a college administrator who used to teach physics. One day when we were talking, we both had a flash of insight about, well, the Insight Factor. Once he understood the idea of *insight*, he used his technical knowledge to compare insight to light. You may not know that the light we see is both a wave and a particle.

As a particle (called a photon), light can hit other particles and collide within atoms. Insight works the same way. When insight collides with our awareness, we get a flash of inspiration or awareness. It affects our internal worlds instantly.

But light is also a wave. It reflects and refracts against the objects in our environment, creating colors and textures, and making everything visible. Even when the biggest light in the sky sets in the evening, the full moon reflects its light to help us see at night. Insight, like light waves, can also affect the external.

Insight works like a wave too. When insight truly affects us, we're able to ride its wave from one good decision to the next — even if the initial insight came from someone else.

Insight is truth that builds on itself, whether first- or second-hand. The key is to ride the wave once you feel the particle collide.

Tip 4 - Confront the Truth

Finally, *insight* is enhanced when you confront issues with the truth. For me, my faith is a key factor. Truth comes from knowledge, evaluated experience, and reflecting on the scripture. *"Knowing what is right is like deep water in the heart; a wise person draws from the well within."* [24] That's a perfect description of insight when we confront the truth. Noted author and pastor Mark Batterson extends this thought, *"Who can calculate the opportunity costs when we ignore the promptings of the Spirit, thereby missing divine appointments?* He is talking about the value of reflection. *"He then adds, "Faith is not faith until it is acted on."* [25]

Whether you are a person of faith or not, may I encourage you to deliberately work to develop your insight? Adopt a 'what if' mindset. Be still and listen. Be open to a flash of insight and recognize when to act.

*   *   *

Insight Questions for Teams

There is no better way to garner insight than by asking the right questions. You can ask specific questions to engage foresight, hindsight, and engage-sight with your team.

1. What are the needs?

A powerful technique to help identify both the needs of the team and its problems is to write *user stories*. A *user story* helps identify the three critical components of insight: who, what, and why. User stories typically adhere to the following format:

- As a _____ <persona>,
- I want to _____ <need or desire>,
- So that _____ <outcome / value>

User stories provide insight to the team by identifying needs to be supported. Table 1 provides a few examples inspired by the 1936 U.S. Olympic Rowing Team. It's important to note that multiple user stories can be attached to a single role.

Table 1 –User Stories Example

WHO	WHAT	WHY
As a Coach,	I want my team to pace themselves,	So that they have the reserves to finish strong.
As a Coxswain,	I want to know what rate we are rowing,	So that I can lead the team with awareness.
As an Oarsman,	I want to know if I should row faster or slower,	So that we are putting ourselves in the best position to win.
As a Coxswain,	I want to know how the wind and current is impacting us,	So that I can rudder the boat properly.
As an Oarsman,	I want to know how much more we have to go,	So that I can continue to summon the energy to finish the race.

You can use *user stories* to capture almost anything, from discovering the needs of those you serve, to tightening down your team's processes.

A leader who asks the right questions early in the process brings valuable foresight to the team. To help you further in identifying user stories, here are a few questions to consider.

- What is the problem that needs to be solved?
- What is the end state that others would desire?
- What are the strengths of what we could offer? Why is it important?
- Who on the team can help make a difference? Why are they important?
- What things might we be missing to carry out the vision?

2. Who is it for?

The *"Who is it for?"* question is centered on the power of personas.

In examples above, we used the various roles of a rowing team — Coach, Coxswain, and Oarsman — to exemplify the personas of that team. Your team's personas will look different but act the same in the user story.

A persona should contain enough information to characterize the type of users interested in your product or service. Your goal is to get into the persona's mind and build empathy with the role.

The Persona Template

While the user story template earlier provided a powerful medium, here's a template that you can use to further capture personas.

Table 2 – The Persona Template

Attribute	Notes
Persona Type	
Defining Characteristics	
Likes and Dislikes	
How they use the product, or value the service	
Their goals and desires	

Use the Persona Template for each one of the stakeholders related to your team to create a better understanding of their needs and wants.

3. What do you like? What do you wish was different?

Questions lead to understanding, and my favorite two questions for garnering feedback that support both hindsight and engage-sight are:

- What do you like?
- What do you wish was different?

The first question draws in the affirmative, uplifting characteristics that others on the team need to stay united.

The second question asks for candid feedback in such a way that few will feel criticized. These questions are intended to help create a circle of safety for the team and prompt ideas focused on continuous improvement.

4. How can we do it better?

To truly access your team's engage-sight, you must go a little deeper. The three questions I like to ask to help create continuous improvement are:

- How are we adding value?
- What can we commit to do better next time?
- How will we be able to deliver or offer it, and when?

*　　*　　*

Key Takeaways

In this chapter we talked about the importance of the Insight Factor of *team strong leadership*. Gaining insight takes practice. You must practice **foresight**, **hindsight**, and **engage-sight** if you want an insightful team.

Ed Catmull, the cofounder of Pixar and the current CEO of Disney Animation, is a great example of a leader who constantly seeks insight from others. He shares, *"It isn't enough merely to be open to ideas from others. Engaging the collective brainpower of the people you work with is an active, ongoing process. As a manager, you must coax ideas out of your staff and constantly push them to contribute."* [26]

Catmull's words offer us a real-world example of the Insight Factor of *team strong leadership*. If you consider the success Catmull's teams have had with Pixar and Disney, you'll realize that what he has accomplished is significant. For Catmull, *breaking average* is best achieved by harvesting insight. As leaders and teams, we ought to do the same.

Chapter 5 - The Collaboration Factor

FEATURING GLORIA BURGESS

"Unity is strength...
when there is teamwork and collaboration,
wonderful things can be achieved."
— Mattie Stepanek

When it comes to teamwork, Henry Ford said it best. *"If everyone is moving forward together, then success takes care of itself."* Ford, who built an entire industry by bringing the efficiency of mass production to automobile manufacturing, and who was all about *breaking average* as an innovator, is talking about the importance of collaboration.

Collaboration is a critical factor for any team because collaboration creates chemistry. Chemistry is that feeling of oneness that occurs among people you spend quality time with.

Consider another massive company that may be *breaking average* right before our eyes: Chick-fil-A. The culture of collaboration that they have created with their employees — and their customers — is legendary. [27] Next time you go to a Chick-fil-A watch how the team executes their roles. Watch for the chemistry. It's not the industry average, is it?

Chick-fil-A Collaboration

A few years ago, I had a chance to connect with Dan Cathy, the CEO of Chick-fil-A. I wanted to know how they built their culture of collaboration and chemistry.

He shared that in the early years, the Chick-fil-A executive leadership team visited the Disney organization and went through a study of the *"Disney approach to people management."* [28] They learned that leading by example is a storyline that always delivers tangible results. These results include things like *"improved behavior and increased productivity."* Those two words stuck out to me: behavior and productivity.

It occurred to me that if you want productive team members, you have to establish the behavior you want from them. Cathy shared that *"culture is reflected by demonstrating the behaviors that your team **values**."* He added that, as a leader, *"you have to teach this — model this to your own team."*

Think about the importance of values. In Chapter 3, we talked about another "V" word, vision, but we also talked about how to get to your vision — and that's through knowing your values. If the team shares values, you're one step of the way to a culture of chemistry.

After hearing the insights from Dan Cathy, I went home and looked up Chick-fil-A*'s* values. They have five: [29]

1. Customer First
2. Personnel Excellence
3. Continuous Improvement
4. Working Together
5. Stewardship

Their fourth value, "Working Together", speaks of the importance of collaboration. But the other values are behaviors modeled from the team that also encourage collaboration.

Collectively, they create and establish a culture focused on *breaking average.*

Many people have said a lot about culture, and for good reason. Culture is more important than vision because culture is the one value shared by every team member. Vision, on the other hand, is fostered by the leader.

You know your team has culture when you witness patterns of collaboration. Remember, collaboration is about chemistry. And where you have chemistry, you have culture. As author Daniel Coyle shares, the word "culture" comes from the Latin word *cultus,* which means *care.* [30] I can't think of a better way to describe an authentic culture than this: that you care for one another.

Chemistry is the evidence of culture in play when a team is rooted in a clear set of values.

One absolutely critical value to having a healthy culture is belonging. Everyone — young or old, rich or poor — wants to know they belong. Chemistry through collaboration happens when people feel like they belong to a family of people with similar values.

When people have that sense of belonging, they don't want to let anyone down. They want to be there for each other. Another word for chemistry is comradery. Comradery is *"a feeling of friendliness, goodwill, and familiarity among the people in a group."* [31]

Now let's look at what it takes to cultivate collaboration that fosters chemistry.

The Elements of Collaboration

Collaboration starts with the leader but needs to be reciprocated by the contributors of the team. To establish collaboration, leaders must pursue three essential elements:

1. Collaboration happens when there is first a commitment to **communicate** by the leader.
2. Collaboration happens when there is a spirit of **cooperation** modeled by the contributors on the team.
3. Collaboration happens when there is a common desire for the team to **interact**.

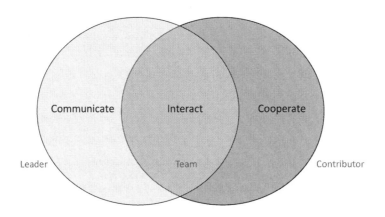

Collaboration

Figure 4 – The Collaboration Factor

When you see the three elements of the Collaboration Factor in play, you know you have a strong team with chemistry.

Work to Communicate

The first element to collaboration is to **communicate**. Communication relies upon the leader to initiate. So, what does a leader need to communicate to their team? The most critical elements to share are the needs, the values, the vision, and the progress.

But before communicating these elements, seek to understand your team. What are their needs, values, doubts, fears? When you seek to understand first, it's easier for you to be understood. The best way to communicate your understanding is to be empathetic.

Next, remember the importance of messaging. Employees don't want to be in the dark. They want a sense of belonging. They want to be contributors. Your job as a leader is to enlighten them, encourage them, and challenge them.

Finally, communicate according to the rules of *breaking average*. Unlike in typical settings, when you encourage *team strong leadership*, the chain of command shouldn't dictate the flow of communication to be just top down. Instead, it should do the opposite: it should open up the potential for communication across all levels, no matter who you are. For *team strong leadership* the chain of command is used predominantly to offer a clear path of support for decision making; it should never be used as a rod that restricts communication.

The Legacy of Communication

A fitting example of collaboration — and how communication triggers it — centers again upon Chick-Fil-A. Twenty years before Chick-fil-A ever existed, Dan's father Truett Cathy opened a restaurant called the Dwarf House, south of Atlanta. His restaurant wasn't known for chicken, though. It was known for hamburgers and steaks. *(Shh... Don't tell that to the Chick-Fil-A cows.)*

But in 1964, Truett was offered a sweet deal on an overstock of chicken breasts from a local poultry supplier. Seizing the moment, Truett took the order, ending up with more chicken than what he knew he what to do with. He then went to work and devised a new cooking method to serve his patrons a fresh option on the menu — the chicken sandwich. Truett realized he had a winning recipe with the chicken and eventually launched a new restaurant dedicated almost entirely to his new creation: Chick-fil-A. The rest is history.

Chick-fil-A's success is due largely in part to the communication model they built from Truett's first storefront. A few years ago, I had a chance to see first-hand the preparation they put into their annual owner-operators meeting. At this event, they bring in every single operator of over 2,400 stores across the country. It's a massive undertaking, but what's striking is that communication is the key to the whole event. This includes communication with team members, operators, customers, and even members of the communities that they serve.

Both internally and externally, Chick-fil-A takes communication seriously. Dan Cathy shares, *"You cannot delegate others to teach culture to your team. It has to come from you."* Communication isn't what you say, it's what you do.

At the end of the day, the best way to communicate is with action, not just words. Your values must be modeled to your team if they're going to buy in and begin creating a culture of chemistry.

Dan Cathy believes that *"leadership is 80 percent of what you do and 20 percent of what you say."* Culture and chemistry are born from that type of communication.

Choose to Cooperate

Soon after Chick-fil-A started, Truett and his leadership team realized they had a scalable model that could be replicated. The next step was to create clear guidelines on how their stores should operate. They knew they needed others to help "co-operate" each of those stores. That meant they needed to equip them.

When you say the word "cooperate" at normal speed, you may lose some of its meaning. I wrote "co-operate" on purpose, though. When you say it slower, almost as two words, doesn't it make more sense?

The word's origins help solidify its meaning. The word "cooperate" comes from two distinct Latin words: *"co"*, which means "together", and *"operari"*, which means "to work."

As we can see from its etymology, collaboration can't truly happen without people working together. In this book, we've been calling these people contributors. Cooperation by contributors multiplies the values of the organization.

Chick-fil-A has a strong understanding of the power of contributors. Their contributors include owner-operators. An owner-operator invests $10,000 of their own money to start a new store, and if they pass the stringent evaluation to ensure they represent the company's culture authentically, they are given the go-ahead and necessary training for free. They are even given the support and financial resources to build their restaurant and launch a store. It's a perfect example of cooperation.

Look to Interact

When you have leaders that communicate and contributors that cooperate, you begin to see the potential for collaboration. But there is one more piece to the puzzle — leaders and team members must look to **interact**. Interaction creates sustained collaboration, resulting in new ideas, and team chemistry.

I'm fortunate to have several Chick-fil-A stores near my home. Years ago, a team member for one of the stores in town came up with a special sauce that brought a new, distinct flavor to the famous chicken sandwich. For years, that special sauce could only be found at one store: the Spotsylvania Mall Chick-fil-A in Fredericksburg, Virginia. Through deep interaction with team members and customers, the operator, Hugh Fleming, perfected it. As a customer, I still remember the little unlabeled cups they served it in.

Eventually, word spread about the amazing sauce, and the company's leadership began to interact with Fleming and copackers (there is that word *"co"* again), who could mass produce the sauce and make it available at all their locations. You now know it by its official name: Chick-fil-A® Sauce.

The secret sauce, however, isn't so secret. It's a medley of other sauces, including honey, barbeque, mustard and ranch dressing. You could probably make it at home if you wanted. But secret or not, that sauce would have never come to life if it wasn't for the **interaction** between an operator and the contributing members of his team. Think of how much collaboration took place to bring this special sauce to the world:

- A team member and an operator interacted to hone the recipe.
- The operator and team members interacted with customers to get valuable feedback. (I was one of them).
- The leadership of Chick-fil-A interacted with the operator and co-packers to come up with a method to scale and distribute it.
- The leadership interacted with every Chick-fil-A operator in America to offer their patrons the same special sauce.

The bottom line is that there's power in interaction. As leaders, it's important not to dismiss or avoid it. And as contributors, it's important to interact with both your leaders and your colleagues because it creates a sense of belonging.

A Coach's Insight

WITH GLORIA BURGESS

Gloria Burgess is an accomplished author, speaker, and coach. She shared a beautiful illustration related to the Collaboration Factor and has allowed me to share it with you.

*　　*　　*

My husband John and I love music. John, in fact, is a conductor. Because of this, we are occasionally invited to events that combine the arts with leadership. What I find fascinating is that the arts provide a vocabulary that the business world doesn't normally use. Collaboration is a critical factor in both composing and making music and is fundamentally the same as collaboration in business.

Think of the instruments in an orchestra. Individual pieces and players magically blend together to offer something that moves us physically, emotionally, and maybe even spiritually.

Leaders can orchestrate the same type of collaboration with our teams. In an orchestra, the conductor communicates with every facial expression and every wave of their arm. For the music to be heard, the orchestra must cooperate with the conductor and with each other. The key here is that the conductor isn't playing just one instrument. No. Instead, they are relying on the contributors — the orchestra members — to play the instruments. The interaction we see here is fully centered on chemistry.

*　　*　　*

Collaboration Tips for Leaders

As leaders, we must "conduct" our team's collaboration to create chemistry. Here are a few tips to jump-start your team's collaboration.

Tip 1 - Ask the Right Questions

Questions are the most engaging form of communication you can have. Here are a some of my favorites to engage collaboration:

- What needs can we support?
- Who is willing to take on the task?
- How can we add value to others?

Tip 2 - Take Time to Listen

What I learned from Gloria's example is that an orchestra conductor is always listening. He or she is acutely aware of every instrument, every note, every contributor in the orchestra. Through subtle gestures, they signal the contributors to let them know when, how fast, and how loudly to play.

In the same way, leaders have to learn to listen. It's critical. When we learn to listen, we are better at leading.

Tip 3 - Keep up the Tempo

Music flows. It has rhythm. As the leader, you're the conductor of your team, and you must maintain the tempo. The best conductors — and the best musicians — know that even if the tune is off, or someone's playing at the wrong time, you keep going. You can't stop the orchestra if one person's slightly off-pace. Instead, you adjust and keep going. You press on. The key is to know and maintain the tempo of the overall team.

If you're able to keep the tempo, the challenges your team will face will be easier. A rough spot or a troubled task won't solve itself if the leader stops the whole team. No, as musicians know, if something didn't sound quite right, or you screw up your part, you just go on. You can only adjust by playing the next note, the next part. Leading a team is no different.

Hesitancy from either the leader or a contributor can derail the team. On the other hand, shared perseverance will unite your team and create the chemistry you need for true collaboration.

Tip 4 - Learn to Laugh Together

Just as music can provide an emotional connection with an audience, so can laughter. I remember enjoying good laughs with the sports teams that I played on growing up. Those moments were an important step in uniting us. This was especially true for those teams I was a part of that found success and won a few championships. Laughter helped us ride through tough losses, and laughter helped gel us for big wins. As I look back, I have great memories of being a part of winning teams that had great chemistry — and I remember laughter being a key part of it.

Robert Orbin, an investment advisor, captured the importance of laughter on teams beautifully. He said, *"If you can laugh together, you can work together."* I love this thought because it's a reminder to find moments to laugh with your team. Laughter unites the team, spurs collaboration, and creates chemistry.

Collaboration Questions for Teams

I shared earlier three Right Questions that the leader can use to help center your team on collaboration; they were basically What? Who? and How? questions. But it's not just the leaders who can foster collaboration. Your team can use these questions as well, with some guidance.

Going back to Gloria's illustration, a leader is like an orchestra conductor. An orchestra combines different instruments from different families to play a single piece of music. The different instruments include:

- string instruments like the violin, viola and cello
- brass instruments like the trumpet and trombone
- woodwinds like the flute and clarinet
- percussion instruments like the bass drum and xylophone

Your team is like this blend of different instrument families. As the conductor, your job is to influence all the musicians playing different instruments to work together. You may have realized, though, that it's not all on you. It's also on the musicians themselves. They need to know the What, Who, and How of collaboration if they are to play well together.

In order for your team to benefit from the feedback, you need them to feel empowered to share through the power of questions. You may hear a few trivial gripes or complaints, but you will also hear insight and wisdom. If you want true collaboration, allow all kinds of questions to be asked to spur and ignite your contributors to action.

Specifically, take a moment to consider the following questions to create collaboration with your team.

1. What is our Definition of Done?

To ensure co-operation (and transparency), team members need to have a shared understanding of what done looks like before the start of an effort. By asking, *"what is our Definition of Done?"*, the team knows when a project can be considered complete. Otherwise, you risk team members having different views and attitudes of what is considered "done."

Each team's Definition of Done can be different for various projects or endeavors. Besides building collaboration, having a shared Definition of Done also creates a sense of ownership. It builds confidence in the team because they have a clear idea of what should be done and when. We'll talk more about this in Chapter 7 — The Ownership Factor.

2. What's our Work Backlog?

A *work backlog* is the list of everything that is needed or wanted for a project, product, or pursuit. Think of it as the organization-wide "to-do" list. Each item in the backlog represents valuable work, though some items are clearly more valuable than others — or needed sooner. Therefore, no team should feel the pressure of accomplishing everything in the work backlog. Some items are more pressing than others. Once you've captured everything your organization wants to accomplish by asking, *"What's our work backlog?"*, the next step is to pare down the list.

3. What's our Sprint Backlog?

A *sprint* is a block of time, set by the team, to accomplish specific work backlog items. A single sprint may last anywhere from a week to a month — the length doesn't matter as long as it's defined and agreed to at the start.

The *sprint backlog* is a limited subset of work backlog items selected for a sprint. It can be the most urgent items, the most important items, or a team's specific goals.

By asking, *"What's our sprint backlog?"*, teams can work together to identify everything they can accomplish in the time specified. This results in a plan for delivering the project, product or pursuit.

4. What's our MVP?

When evaluating a product or service to be created, the team can collaborate by deciding what the *Minimum Viable Product (MVP)* should be. The focus of the MVP is on trimming the sprint backlog. By asking, *"What's our MVP?"*, you can help the team reevaluate the sprint backlog plan and determine two important elements:

a) Is there something in the sprint backlog that doesn't need to be there?

b) Is there something from the work backlog that should be in the current sprint backlog?

Asking about the MVP helps eliminate waste, so that the team can get to producing and delivering something of value faster.

One technique to identify your MVPs is called the MoSCoW technique. I learned this powerful evaluation trick from Chris Li, an Agile coach and Certified Scrum Trainer. The letters MSCW (hence, MoSCoW) represent four priorities to evaluate your sprint backlog. [32]

Table 3 – The MoSCoW Template

	Priorities		Item(s)
M	Must have	Required to be a success, therefore critical to the sprint.	
S	Should have	Important but not necessary for the current sprint plan.	
C	Could have	Desirable, but not necessary, could offer good "bang for the buck" and could be included if time allows.	
W	Won't have	Least critical item. It has the lowest payback, and not part of the current sprint plan.	

Use the ITEM(s) column with your team to identify each backlog item under consideration. In the end, your MVP will be the items in row M, and perhaps some of row S. If your team achieves all these, they can then move to row C.

5. Who's Got What?

Following the trimming, a *sprint backlog* that has been groomed with a vision for what will be delivered or completed as reflected by the MVP. Now the team can focus on identifying who will accomplish each part.

The question for assigning team members to tasks is simple: *"Who's got what?"* or, *"Who's responsible?"*

Think back to the orchestra example that Gloria shared. There are many instruments and different parts of the music must be played by different musicians. With a finalized sprint backlog, you know what item is expected, like a sound in the orchestra, but you may not know who will deliver it.

To solve this ambiguity, each sprint backlog item should be assigned to a specific team member. The key is determining who is best able to play the right role for certain tasks. By asking *"Who's got what?"*, the team gets clarity on what everyone is doing for each sprint backlog item, and the best part is that people can volunteer themselves!

Tasking is how a group of musicians become a band, and it's how a group of contributors become a team.

6. How is it Going — Seriously?

Invariably, most people have a standard response to the staple small-talk question: *"How's it going?"* What do you normally say? *"Fine,"* or *"I'm good."* By itself, it's not a terrible question, but the true intent behind it is rarely there. Yet, it should still be asked — just in a more authentic way.

Based on the previous question, *"Who's got what?"* — it should be clear what needs to be done, and who needs to do it. *"How's it going"* is a question for the team to collaborate on a daily basis during the project or effort. I've found "stand-up" meetings to be especially effective if you can have them —daily, if possible.

A stand-up meeting is used among Agile software development teams, but the concept is scalable for any team and for any project. It's not limited to just software. For your stand-ups, require your team to be on time and don't let anyone sit — seriously. Encourage your team to share brief updates and keep the meeting short. Start on time and end on time.

At each stand-up, every person on the team should answer three quick questions regarding their progress on their tasks:

- What have you been working on since we last met?
- What are you planning to work on next?
- Is there anything getting in the way of keeping you from making progress?

These three questions are a more genuine way to ask your team *"How's it going?"* They also offer many benefits, such as the following:

- It keeps the team engaged
- It creates a sense of accountability
- It provides a safe environment for team members to get help
- It keeps one person from being overburdened
- It allows the leaders to be more attentive and empathetic
- It encourages team members to stay committed and communicate their needs
- It creates a sense of belonging

Any of the six collaboration questions are powerful and can help a team become better. Using them gets you closer to experiencing VICTORY.

*   *   *

Key Takeaways

In this chapter, we talked about the importance of collaboration. Collaboration starts with the leader and is reciprocated by the contributors. *Team strong leaders* must **communicate** effectively. And *team strong contributors* need to **cooperate** with chemistry. Effective communication is more likely when the leader ties the team to the vision, sharing the vision through their values. When the leader has communicated and the team begins to cooperate, you can ultimately create an environment where everyone is allowed to **interact**.

As business expert Jim Collins shares in his book *Good to Great,* the important thing is to get the right people on the bus and in the right seats. This is a great analogy for true collaboration.

When the right people are in the right seats and the bus is moving in the right direction, you have a collaborative team.

For this to happen, the whole team must know what needs to be done, who's doing what, how everyone is doing, and what the Definition of Done is.

You can't *break average* without collaboration. Steve Jobs reminds us, *"Great things in business are never done by one person. They're done by a team of people."* Job's words are a powerful reminder of the Collaboration Factor of *team strong leadership*. Though Jobs is easily credited as one of the most famous modern business leaders with his success at Apple, it's clear what he did was achieved through the power of collaboration. And as his quote reminds us, collaboration is a critical component to *breaking average*.

Chapter 6 - The Trust Factor

FEATURING JAY JOHNSON

"Trust doesn't mean that you trust that someone won't screw up— it means you trust them even when they do screw up."
— *Ed Catmull*

A lynchpin factor that is needed for teamwork is *trust*. Trust creates **confidence**. It creates confidence in ourselves, and confidence in our teammates. When a team has trust, there is belief that each team member can be relied upon, and there is faith that the team will prevail in the end.

The best way to build trust, according to Patrick Lencioni, *"is to overcome our need for invulnerability."* Invulnerability is a desire to be sheltered from harm or damage. It's this desire for invulnerability that can keep us from pursuing life and truly engaging with others. We can't live that way.

Shedding this desire for invulnerability helps leaders gain the awareness they need to empower and lead a team and gain their trust.

While as leaders we can't offer a risk free, challenge free environment, we can build a culture that offers each member of the team protection and immunity from being chastised or ridiculed for their ideas, suggestions, or service.

Teamwork is about being vulnerable and taking risks, yet knowing we have the support of others. It's not about being risk-averse, it's about being risk-tolerant.

"12 Strong" Trust

The movie *12 Strong* demonstrates this type of trust. It is based on the real-life events following the tragedy of 9/11. In this story, a group of 12 men are part of a Special Forces Team deployed to Afghanistan. [33]

What we see unfold is a young leader who is asked to take the Special Forces Team on a combat mission that has little chance of success. To make matters worse, this young leader has never led other soldiers into battle before. He's green. Despite his inexperience, he knows he can count on two things: trust and training. Trust is what gives him and his teammates confidence.

It is through the process of trust — overcoming the default desire for invulnerability — he is able to face impossible odds, unite his team, and make connections with local Afghan citizens to accomplish a harrowing mission against the Taliban. Using what resources they can find through the power of trust, they are able to contest the enemy and find victory. It's a mesmerizing story rich with the Trust Factor.

In this chapter, we will explore further what it takes to cultivate this type of trust. We will talk about how to build rock solid trust as a leader, and how to maintain a high level of trust among the team.

The Elements of Trust

There are three essential elements of trust that a leader and his team must pursue in order to create *team strong confidence*; first the leader must be **credible.** Second, the contributors must be **dependable**. When those two things happen then it allows us to reach the third element — it allows the team to be **serving**.

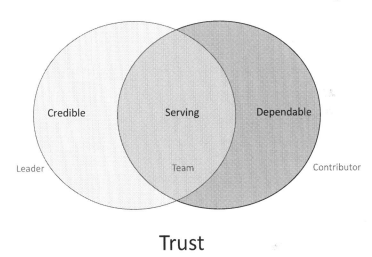

Trust

Figure 5 – The Trust Factor

You can't have integrity and *team strong leadership* without trust. The three elements for the Trust Factor establish confidence for a team and its members.

Stay Credible

The first element to trust is to be **credible**. Let's be real. It's tough to fully trust someone who lacks credibility. Those people can talk a good game, can say all the right things, but if there is a lack of congruence between their words and deeds, then credibility vanishes.

What does it mean to be credible? Credibility is the quality of being trusted and believed in. Credible means you are authentic. You practice what you preach. You are someone who believes in themselves and in those around them. You deliver results, not just empty promises. You are transparent. And you are not afraid to face tough decisions.

Credible leaders are not perfect, nor do they try to be. Instead, they strive for excellence, being real, and taking action. They are genuine and honest in the way they conduct themselves, and the way they interact with others.

So, here's a key question. Would you consider yourself a credible leader? If you were to rank your credibility, what would it be?

It's believed most leaders, if they were honest, would recognize that there's always room for improvement.

The good news is, credibility is a lever that you can control and adjust. You can easily increase your credibility if you choose too. It simply requires intentional effort and time.

Credibility through Consistency

One way a leader can increase their credibility is to be consistent. Let's face it, it's hard for a leader to be viewed as credible if they act one way around one group of people and a different way in other groups. If people don't know who they're getting or the values they're going to see on display from day-to-day, they'll quickly become confused and your credibility will decrease.

Consistency goes a long way to building credibility. The best way to improve in this area is to be the same person with every group you are with; be yourself with everyone.

Credibility through Candor

Another area a leader can increase their credibility is by being a person of candor. Candor means you care. It's difficult to be a credible leader if you don't offer candor. If you placate others by telling them what you think they want to hear, rather than what they truly need to hear, then you miss a great opportunity to lead.

Placating people — hiding things under the surface — makes it tough for a leader to be trusted. William Shakespeare reminds us that, *"no legacy is so rich as honesty."* While we don't want to hurt people's feelings, we can still learn to be gentle with candor, and encourage others with loving feedback.

Candor aids our credibility. When you are credible through candor the team will be willing to not just follow your instructions, but to truly believe in what they are doing. Credibility is what trust looks like, but there's more.

Be Dependable

The second element to trust is to be **dependable**. Leaders who do what they say they are going to do and deliver consistent results also earn a reputation as dependable. The same thing can be said for the contributors. Dependability is the hallmark of trust.

If team members demonstrate that they are someone who is dependable it serves as an actuator for the most important element in any relationship…trust. People are drawn to those who follow through and meet expectations. We want them on our team. Few are more trustworthy.

Consider the African Proverb that says, *"if you want to go fast, go alone. If you want to go far, go together."* A leader can't go far unless they have a team they can depend upon.

When you combine credibility and dependability, it spawns the next element of the Trust Factor: a team that is all about serving.

Continue to Serve

The third element to trust is to be **serving**. Have you ever noticed that trustworthy teams seem to be a group of individuals who reflect a culture of service? Their skills and position might be different, but the great teams truly care about serving one another. Why is that?

It always starts with the leader. A leader who believes in the team, and sees each person as a key contributor, sets the tone of service. Yet, a culture of service isn't complete until the contributors have seen that they work for a servant leader. That's when contributors buy into the leader. It all starts with leaders exhibiting a behavior of care and support for others. When this happens, you no longer have a group of isolated individuals, but instead a caring, well-oiled machine, a team, operating as one.

Consider the alternative. Have you ever had a leader say to you, *"Do as I say and not as I do?"* How did that make you feel? Loved? Appreciated? Valued?

I'm guessing probably none of those.

We want to follow leaders who are willing to go where they are asking us to go too. It's impossible to truly trust someone who is encouraging you to do something they are not willing to do themselves.

As previously stated, trust is earned, and we must be vulnerable. One of the best ways to earn trust is by showing others you care and that you are in the fight alongside them. When you serve others, you are demonstrating your belief in the cause and that you are all in with them — and for them.

Servant leaders don't view themselves as holier than thou or better than anyone. In fact, they understand their top priority is to cast vision, train, equip, and clear the path for those they're charged to lead so the team can execute their job or mission in the best possible way.

So why don't more leaders lead with a servant heart? There are several reasons. One is because it isn't what leaders have experienced from other leaders in their own journey. People do what people see. Most have seen bosses, not leaders. They've seen people bark orders, express little concern for others, or someone who may view team members only as a means to what they want and who will make them look good.

The bottom line is this. Trust is earned through acts of service. Trust requires you to give more than you take. Givers gain trust because they consistently demonstrate their willingness to put the needs of others before their own.

Serving others, exemplifies a variety of *team strong leadership* factors, but most importantly it creates strong *trust*.

A Coach's Insight

WITH JAY JOHNSON

To dive deeper, I asked my good friend Jay Johnson, who is an accomplished speaker, to share some of his experiences related to the Trust Factor. Jay is an Air Force veteran who continues to exemplify a life of service.

*   *   *

As a retired United States Air Force officer, and a coach and speaker who is passionate about leadership and equipping others, I've seen first-hand the value of trust. Trust creates dependability.

When I think of dependability, I immediately think of our nation's sentries, the men and women of our Armed Forces. As a military veteran, I value and understand the importance of needing and being able to rely on members of the team. A team without trust is like a plane without fuel. You won't be able to take off, but even if you could, you wouldn't go far. Trust is the fuel every team needs.

Trust Comes with Expectations

Teams are successful because of the trust they've placed in one another. Let me share with you three examples: two from the military and one story for you sports fans.

Example #1

When a precision airstrike is needed, those on the ground are depending on those deploying the munitions to do two things: to be on time and to be on target. Both the forward observer on the ground, and the air strike group need to be dependable. Everything is centered on trust.

Example #2

When military personnel are going to be extracted from an area, the members on the ground are told to be at a specific location on a specific day, at a specific time for pick up. The extraction team is trusting that they will be ready to go when they arrive. At the same time, the ground team is equally counting on and depending on those that promised to be there to extract them. Trust is a two-way street. Both the ground force and the extraction team need to be dependable.

Example #3

When a quarterback calls a pass play, he is depending on his offensive linemen to block and give him time to find an open receiver. Additionally, the quarterback is also counting on the receivers to run the correct routes.

The bottom line is that teams are successful because of the trust they've placed in one another to fulfill their respective roles for the collective good of the team.

Trust Comes Through Vulnerability

Here's the truth. You can't have trust without vulnerability. When we trust in others, we expose ourselves to potential risk, but it's a risk we have to take to accomplish the mission.

My best memory of trust and vulnerability happened on a diving experience a few years back.

Five of us stood on the shore of the Adriatic Sea in Northern Italy. We were discussing our dive plan, inspecting our gear, and suiting up. Our plan was to buddy up for a 30-minute dive. Having a dive buddy was important; a key safety measure should a need arise. Your buddy is someone who helps keep tabs on you and vice versa.

I remembered entering the Adriatic; we stayed on the surface for about 30 yards offshore. To warn boats and other divers, we posted a dive flag. After checking our gear one last time, we put in our regulators, released the air in our vests, and then descended into the depths of the sea.

The water was murky with visibility maybe 10 feet at best. We quickly reached the seabed and followed it slowly away from shore reaching a depth of about 70 feet. We saw a few fish here, an octopus there, but it was mostly a bland environment.

Fifteen minutes into our dive I looked at my gauge and saw that I was consuming far more oxygen than I should have at this point. I realized I might be in danger. I knew I couldn't stay down much longer because I needed to ensure I had enough air during my ascent to properly decompress and release the nitrogen that had built up in my body during the dive. The fear of running out of oxygen ignited a moment of panic.

I quickly tapped my dive buddy, Kevin, on the leg to show him my gauge so that he knew my dive time had been cut short. Kevin looked at my gauge, but, oddly, he simply waved it off and turned to continue his trek. Because I trusted him, my panic subsided temporarily. *"Okay, no big deal,"* I thought, *"I can go a bit more."*

Minutes later, though, I looked at the gauge and grew worried again. It was getting dangerously low. I tapped Kevin's leg a second time, showing him my gauge. I then gave him a thumbs up sign indicating I needed to surface immediately. Once again Kevin waved me off and pressed on. I was dumbfounded, but I knew he was a more experienced diver, and I trusted him. So, I tried to let it go. But I couldn't.

Shortly later, panic struck again as I felt like I was near my last few breaths. I was going to have to surface with or without my dive buddy. I tapped Kevin's leg one more time, showing him my gauge and making it clear I needed to go. I remember wondering why he was not understanding my concern. Finally, Kevin responded to my plight, but it wasn't quite what I expected.

Kevin showed me his gauge. He still had quite a bit of air in it. I remember thinking, *he must be a fish*. What he did next blew me away. Kevin took off his secondary airline and offered it to me. In the depths of the ocean, he gave me a lifeline.

By him choosing to be vulnerable — giving up some of his air — he created what I call "next level trust" with me. My anxiety quickly vanished, and we were able to stay underwater for another 10 minutes, while both breathing on his tank of air.

When Kevin invited me to go diving, I already trusted him. However, it was his act of vulnerability in the midst of my panic that took it to another level. It was that trust that calmed me on that dive, even during the moments of uncertainty. That is what the Trust Factor does. Leaders who choose to be vulnerable with others create trust that lasts a lifetime.

Trust Is a Team's Most Powerful Weapon

I have had the privilege of not only deep-sea diving but also working and serving in various industries and in various countries all around the world. From humble beginnings working in the grocery industry where I managed a department of 10 people by age 18; followed by nearly 22 years in uniform as an enlisted Airman and Officer in the United States Air Force; five years as government civil servant, and now over five years owning and operating my coaching, training, speaking and consulting company. I've seen teams succeed with trust, and also teams fail miserably.

With trust, teams can outperform the average, but without trust they underperform. When it comes to *breaking average*, trust is a team's most powerful weapon.

Trust Tips for Leaders

Teams that fully trust one another seem to operate with a freedom and awareness that others simply cannot fathom. They are resilient, they are comfortable being uncomfortable, and they freely express ideas and respectfully challenge the actions and positions of others without fear of offending or leaving anyone feeling disenfranchised.

Here are a few tips I want to share to help you create a culture where your team can develop the kind of trust that championship teams possess.

Tip 1 - Give Trust to Earn Trust

Credibility starts by recognizing that trust is both given and earned. When you are seen as credible there is a willingness amongst the team to not just follow your instructions, but to truly believe in what they are doing for you. It starts with you being credible, but the fastest way to earn long-term trust is to give it in return.

Think about it. When you first arrive on the scene, more likely than not, you are going to be seen as credible. Some may withhold judgement until after you have proven yourself worthy of leading them, but many people trust by default. We all want to trust in the leader in front of us.

The process for you as a leader starts by recognizing that trust must be reciprocated. If they see you as credible quickly, you need to see them as credible just as quickly. If over time, you are not seen as credible, the fewer will believe in you and a greater number will be reluctant to follow you. Remember, to earn trust, you must give trust.

Tip 2 - Evaluate Trust Levels

Trust happens when it's given and earned. You know you have mutual trust when the team has gone the extra mile.

Here are some useful questions to evaluate trust:

- Are members of the team competent and respected?
- Do members of the team willingly own and admit their shortcomings and mistakes?
- Do members keep their word and follow through on promises and assigned tasks?
- Are members willing to forgo their own immediate needs and desires to support other team members?
- Can team members be counted on with large projects as easily as they can small ones?
- What areas or details, if any, cause you concern when considering assigning or delegating tasks?

Tip 3 - Start Small

Trust starts with being credible. If you are not credible, no one will believe in you. So, how do you build credibility?

I recently heard it said, *"trust is earned in drips, but lost in buckets."* That paints a powerful picture, doesn't it? It's so true.

I've always liked Ernest Hemingway's advice, *"the best way to find out if you can trust someone is to trust them."* But when someone is learning how to drive, you most likely aren't going to hand them the keys to a Lamborghini. You are most likely to start them out on an older car, one that if something happens to the car during the learning process it won't cost you a small fortune to fix.

In the same way, if you were teaching someone to fly, you wouldn't start them out in a Boeing 777. As you begin to trust your team members, give them small, yet meaningful tasks to do so they can demonstrate their trustworthiness. Those who are truly adept and hungry for more will quickly take responsibility, complete their task, and signal their willingness to want more.

The pace at which you give trust and increase responsibility will vary from person to person. Some may quickly move from a walk to a sprint, while others will need a little more time walking and jogging before they are ready to be trusted at a wide-open sprint.

Tip 4 - Make It Safe

As leaders, we don't need to beat up people for their ideas, whether good or bad. Instead, we want to be open to all their ideas. Why? Because when a team has the opportunity to share their ideas it creates for them a sense of being truly appreciated and valued. That only happens through trust.

Start by getting your team together at a location away from the office and free from distractions. Let them know one of the primary goals is to help them get to know each other on a deeper, more personal level than they can by merely working alongside one another on projects and tasks for 9 hours a day, 280 days a year.

You, the leader, are going to have to model for your team what it looks, and sounds like to be vulnerable. Generate a few questions that will cause all members to reflect on their biggest wins, biggest disappointments (personal and professional), and lifelong aspirations to include lofty goals they still desire to achieve. Introduce the questions by posting them on screen, a board, or training chart, and then give everyone time to reflect on what they'd like to share. When you are ready to begin, you, as the leader, must go first.

The more transparent and vulnerable you are the more your team members will open up. If someone expresses concern or discomfort, you can bypass them and let them know you will come back to them. As more and more members share, it increases the likelihood that they will eventually warm up to sharing.

I've stood in rooms where some of the most "manly" men have shared deeply personal things that led them and others in the room to shedding tears. It's also not uncommon to have someone say something like, *"I just learned more about my colleague, <insert name of choice here>, in the last several hours than I've learned by working alongside him or her over the last 'X' number of years."*

This is the power of transparency. When people feel safe to share, it magnifies the trust.

Tip 5 - Know Your Strengths

A person who is credible is aware of their strengths and their shortcomings. Notice we didn't use the word faults. None of us are perfect, but that doesn't mean we are flawed. We simply recognize that we are not perfect, but we were perfectly created and gifted with unique talents and abilities.

You are more likely to be thought credible when there is congruence between words (stated intentions) and deeds (action). And when you operate in your areas of strength, you can be assured that the action you are taking will have the greatest chance of impact.

I've always loved this quote by Ralph Waldo Emerson, *"your actions speak so loudly that I cannot hear what you are saying."* Measure that thought with what I heard a pastor once say, *"make no mistake about it, I'm smoking exactly what I'm selling."* Did that catch your attention? I took this to mean, *"I'm living and doing exactly what I'm encouraging and asking you to do."* Knowing your strengths is about living your strengths.

Tip 6 - Give Permission to Challenge

One of the best ways to foster trust is to let members know their opinion, ideas, and experiences are welcome in every conversation. Let them know there are no sacred cows and you aren't looking for — nor do you desire — "yes" men and women (you know, the ones who agree with everything the boss says).

As a leader, you must set this expectation early and reinforce it often. All my years of working in various organizations of varying sizes and missions has led me to realize that most people are wary of speaking up and challenging the opinion of their supervisors or senior leaders.

Why are they wary? One reason I've heard repeated is reprisal. They fear that despite being asked for their opinion if they share a view different from the one stated by their boss it will be held against them and their annual report, yearly bonus, or future promotion opportunities will be affected. The only way to counter this is to consistently set the expectation that such behavior is permitted and then stand firmly behind it. Just commit yourself to not take anything said or shared personally.

The free flow of communication and ideas is what allows people to be themselves and to feel valued. That is freedom and freedom fuels trust.

Tip 7 - Make it Repeatable

One way to reinforce the importance of dependability is to make it repeatable. The first order of business is to recognize it when you see it. Take time to affirm others for their actions. Proper praise creates sequels. People who are praised for their action will do it again and again. Let them know how much you appreciate them and their follow-through.

Also ensure the rest of the team sees you model exactly what it is you are preaching and praising. Remember, if you are not dependable, they won't be dependable.

Tip 8 - Stay Accountable

To be an effective team, each member must be accountable to the others. Accountability fuels dependability. Accountability isn't about catching people when they do something wrong, it's creating a system that praises people for what they are doing right.

As your team sets objectives and key results, make sure others are aware of the objectives, and who owns what. Make sure everyone sees the positive progress they are making towards the objectives and key results. This is the best way to stay accountable in a way that celebrates achievement.

Tip 9 - Serve Them Like Braveheart!

I've worked for far too many leaders who suffered from what my mentor, John C. Maxwell calls 'Destination Disease'. You know, *"I've arrived"* and *"now it's your job to serve me."* Wrong! In my experience, the best leaders serve routinely and as often as absolutely possible.

The business I created is called J2 Servant Leadership, LLC. The "J2" comes from a designation in the military that stands for Joint Intelligence. Whereas the use of "Servant Leadership" is because that is what I aspire to help others live out.

There's an image that comes to mind regarding servant leadership from the movie *Braveheart* that I often share when I am speaking at conferences or conducting company training. In this movie, we observe two very different kinds of leaders juxtaposed: King Edward I, aka Longshanks, of England, and William Wallace, the Scotsman seeking to rally the Scots to stand up for their sovereignty.

In one particular scene, Longshanks is seen up on top of a hill safe and far removed from a battle. He and some of his military commanders and noblemen are watching the fight wage in the valley below. The fighting is intense and the suffering immense.

Longshanks quickly tires of watching and he turns to one of his military commanders and summons the archers. His commander receives the order then asks, *"Beg pardon sire, won't we hit our own troops?"* Longshanks' reply shows how little he cares about his people when he replies, *"Yes, but we'll hit theirs too."* [34]

Contrast Longshanks' character with William Wallace, played by Mel Gibson. In that battle scene, where was Wallace?

You find him standing right in the middle of the fight side by side with his men. He was willing to be vulnerable, whereas Longshanks was trying to be invulnerable. Who do you think gained more trust?

The reason I believe many leaders don't fulfill the role of Servant Leader is that they have a skewed and misguided notion of the word "servant." They falsely assume and believe servant means "subservient": less than or subordinate to others. They may think, *"How can I show myself as subordinate to those I am charged to lead?"*

The word subordinate, when traced back to its Latin origins, means 'slave'. The reality is that leaders are neither subordinate nor a slave to their people, any more than the people in your organization are to you. Leaders and contributors are all part of the same team and serve one another! It's like Paul's story about the 1936 Olympic Rowing Team in Chapter 1.

Tip 10 - Compound the Interest

Trust is earned through serving and delivering. It's like a bank account. Over time you build up more trust with others as you deposit into your account with them through serving and delivering. The more an individual can build up in the account of trust, the more latitude he or she has with others.

Givers gain trust. However, if an individual allows their trustworthiness to be questioned, the bank account can get depleted quickly. The trick is to always leave more room in the account than you are risking in your decisions that affect others. Trust requires you to give more than you take.

Trust Questions for Teams

The best way to get a team focused on a factor like trust is to ask the right questions. But asking the wrong questions can also be the quickest way to create distrust. We need to ask the right questions, at the right time, and in the right way.

Questions make us vulnerable. The truth is we can't establish trust without vulnerability — so we need to ask questions. However, if the questions being asked come across as questioning someone's trustworthiness, then we will have a problem. According to Brené' Brown, *"it's enough to set vulnerability lockdown in motion."* So, our questions need to be smart, simple, and safe. [35]

Here are some of my favorite questions to build trust and connection:

1. Do you mind if I get your viewpoint?
2. What is your opinion?
3. What do you think are our strengths?
4. What do you think are the opportunities?
5. Would you mind helping me?

6. What would you do?
7. What am I missing?
8. What do you recognize as the strengths each contributor brings?

These questions center on seeking permission and showing your interest. The pattern is simple, you value their opinion and are genuinely asking for their viewpoint. The questions themselves are not where the power is, the power is in the listening. If team members learn to genuinely ask these questions, and seek to understand before being understood, they will create a trusting environment.

I encourage you to take a moment to consider these questions to help you individually as a leader, and to help your team create trusting relationships.

*   *   *

Key Takeaways

In this chapter we talked about the importance of the Trust Factor. In order to build trust, the leader must be **credible** by modeling the team's values. Leaders that are dependable show up, but you also need to count on the contributors to be **dependable** too. If a team can't depend on each other — if they can't deliver on what's being asked — then the leader's trust will be broken. It won't matter how great a leader you might be; you also need a team that comes together. Thirdly, a team that embodies trust must be **serving**. They must offer something that adds value! These three elements are what produces *team strong leadership*.

It isn't a stretch to say that trust is perhaps the most important characteristic of a team. While we may have started with Vision, and talked about the value of Insight and Collaboration, *team strong leadership* now rests upon this foundation of Trust. Trust is as important in relationships, as air is to life. It allows the collective body of an organization to breathe and pursue the goal of *breaking average*.

Trust expert David Horsager shares a powerful precept. *"Trust is a confident belief in someone or something. It is the confident belief in an entity: to do what is right, to deliver what is promised, and to be the same every time, whatever the circumstances."* [36]

This quote is a reminder that trust creates confidence. Confidence is what invariably elevates teams and organizations over others. If you are a *team strong leader*, affirm contributors in their actions. If you are a *team strong contributor*, affirm others in their value. Let teammates know they are credible and dependable. Trust is what creates a culture that influences others to serve, and this ultimately reflects a team that is *breaking average*.

Chapter 7 - The Ownership Factor

FEATURING MIKE HARBOUR

> *"Walk in like you own the place."*
> — *Marriott Key Card*

One of the great differentiators that allows an organization to stand head and shoulders above others centers on creating a sense of *ownership* amongst a team. Ownership creates connection. It creates a feeling of oneness for a team, and a spirit of pride.

Consider your favorite sports team. There is likely a tribe of followers, and a nation of fans whose allegiances are with the team throughout the week and throughout the season — especially on game day. That's a sign of connection.

Because of this connection, when the team wins, the tribe of followers will also feel a sense of jubilation. Conversely, when the team loses, the very same followers who have invested time, money or attention into the team will feel pain. Emotionally it's as if they actually own the team.

Connection is what separates the good teams from the great. Build a loyal following, establish a committed team, and you'll go far in creating a sense of ownership.

Now, does everybody really "own" the team? Well you may not think so, but when someone invests time or their hard-earned money on team swag, guess what? They're in. They feel like an owner — at least a minority owner. An entire city can feel that way.

Think of the Green Bay Packers, as an example. Ownership creates connection — especially on game day — and if we are lucky to have seats for the big game, we can't wait to high five and fist bump all the other "owners" at the game. Connections in a group occur when they have a common bond.

Do you know how you can tell when the Ownership Factor is in play for a team? It's when you see a sense of pride amongst the tribe of followers. It's when they go the extra mile. Whereas, when there is no spirit of pride, when a team doesn't have a sense of ownership, you won't see the tribe go the extra mile.

Team strong leadership, to be effective, needs a sense of ownership. Ownership goes a long way in helping team members and their followers feel connected and a part of a tribe.

The Husky Ownership Campaign – The Other Miracle

To understand the power of ownership, let's revisit the 1936 Olympic Gold Medal rowing team highlighted earlier. Would you believe their trip to Berlin almost never happened? Right after the Olympic Trials, the University of Washington Husky crew team was asked to surrender their spot to represent their country despite being the best U.S. team. Why? Because they lacked sufficient funds to make the international journey.

In those days, each team required their own funding to cover their trip to the games. It turned out the University of Washington Husky team lacked the necessary resources. They had spent every dollar that had to make the cross-country trip to the Olympic trials. Little did they know that they would also have to pay their own way to travel to Germany. The crew team, the athletes, the university — none of them had the funds to board the chartered Olympic boat that was reserved and ready to go.

Rather than the Olympic committee stepping in to help, they pushed back and "suggested" that one of the runner-up teams, which had the financial resources, go instead. The Husky team was deflated. One minute it looked like they had their tickets stamped to the Games, the next minute it had been snatched from their hands.

Leaders like Ulbrickson, however, don't give up easily. Dreams are never easy. We often experience challenges to see how bad we really want it. This is where the Ownership Factor comes into play.

There are always two choices when we face a challenge, (a) we can choose to rise up and fight it (own our future), or (b) we can choose to give up and settle for average (let others choose our future for us).

Rather than giving up, Ulbrickson went to work. He believed his team belonged — that they had earned it. Who were they to take their dream away?

In those days, there wasn't a *GoFundMe* page to crowdsource for capital, or the World Wide Web to convey the message on social media. Those things hadn't been invented yet. Instead, Ulbrickson, as their coach, fought the funding requirement by going up against the mighty Olympic Committee. He was given an ultimatum of just a few days to come up with the money or else another team would go in their place.

Somehow word got out about the team's situation. Husky fans, the local media, and the community from across the country pulled together, and by the last minute the team miraculously raised the funds they needed. That's the Ownership Factor in full play. Husky fans, and rowing fans felt connected to that team, and more than that, they felt compelled to help.

Soon, the Husky crew and their coach found themselves on the S.S. Manhattan along with the other U.S. Olympians crossing the Atlantic to Hamburg, Germany. When you help a team out like that, and support such a major goal and lofty aspiration, it's as if you are a member of the team. For the fans and philanthropists that helped pay their way, there is no doubt that they felt like they won the gold medal too. That's the feeling that comes with the Ownership Factor, when the team we root for wins it all.

Intel's Ownership Campaign

The Ownership Factor focuses on creating connections and establishing community. Community can't happen unless there is first a connection. Once there is community, people take on an attitude of responsibility for carrying out the team's mission.

Another great example of this is how Andy Grove, CEO of Intel led his company in *breaking average* in the tech industry. Intel started off as a manufacturer of memory chips. They also had a small hand in creating microprocessors, but that wasn't their bread and butter business. Memory storage was their focus. [37]

Unfortunately, they were getting beat up by Japanese manufacturers in the memory storage business, who were undercutting their cost. They couldn't keep up, and they were financially leaking like a ruptured water pipe.

Sensing the growing dysfunction within his company, which was becoming the average, Grove took ownership of what needed to be done and pivoted the business to focus on microprocessors instead.

As they progressed, new threats emerged. Grove realized they needed to have the team step up their game. With an aggressive schedule, they developed the 8086, which was the world's first commercial 16-bit microprocessor. It had the potential to be a game changer.

There was just one more problem. Based on the insight that he gathered (see Chapter 4 for the Insight Factor), Grove knew few consumers understood the merits and value of this breakthrough microprocessor. Furthermore, it was recognized that the common standard marketing approach often practiced in the tech industry, would not work. Few consumers would see the value. Grove and his team knew that their marketing approach needed to be centered on *breaking average* — just like the microprocessors they had created.

Since their technology filled a need that consumers didn't know they had, the challenge was clear. Andy Groves put out an internal company memo titled *Operation Crush* that would result in a marketing campaign that would revolutionize the way technology would be marketed, used, and understood. [38]

To connect with consumers, Intel branded a marketing solution that focused on the consumer story of how their new chip would benefit and simplify their life. It emphasized the merits — the value it offered — with a minimum level of inconvenience. Operation Crush would make every North American want a PC with the new chip. It's the same marketing strategy Apple uses today to sell their products. The focus isn't on the product per se, it's on the consumer using the product, and how their world changes for the better.

Operation Crush wasn't just a mission to market the strengths and merits of the 8086 processor, it was to show that Intel was *breaking average* for consumers and offering something to the world that they needed to experience. Their marketing approach — not just their technology — was centered on *breaking average*. It was a game changer in its own right.

The Elements of Ownership

How can a leader cultivate a sense of ownership amongst a tribe or a team?

There are three essential elements that a leader must carry out to establish a sense of ownership with others. First, they must **define** the opportunity for others by creating a cause or sharing a challenge. Second, they need to **empower** the tribe to feel as if they have some possession and voice into the team in regard to the mission of *breaking average*. Third, they need to allow the team — including the followers — to be able to **implement** their ideas and help execute the team's mission. These elements go beyond just a sports team or a tech company. They are elements essential for any group or organization.

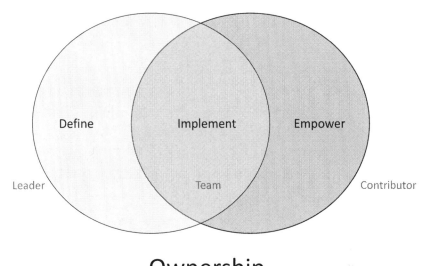

Ownership

Figure 6 – The Ownership Factor

The three elements of the Ownership Factor establish deep connections for a team and a tribe starting with the leader. Let's explore these elements further and evaluate how the Ownership Factor can be a critical component for *breaking average*.

Define the Opportunities

The first thing a leader must do is **define** an opportunity, which is an objective, goal or need. Without clear objectives, it's impossible for others to take ownership — unless you want them to own average.

The entire responsibility of defining the objective isn't squarely on you as the leader. As a leader it's important to allow others to communicate what is needed. Your job as leader is to listen to the ideas, evaluate and analyze the information, and then decide ultimately what objectives should be met. If you don't ultimately take responsibility for validating and approving what is defined, then you risk having a team with no clear direction.

It's not enough to know you have something unique. It's equally important to share your strengths and allow others to be early adopters. You want others to be part of the team. Defining objectives and capability creates that sense of ownership. This is clearly what Andy Groves did for Operation Crush.

Once enacted, Operation Crush created the breakthrough that Intel needed by first clarifying objectives tied to measurable key results. Defining the objectives and key results and getting buy-in from their sales staff to execute Operation Crush, transformed Intel from a tech "wanna be" to the premier technology leader we know in the marketplace today. Little Intel, as they could have been called back then, was focused on *breaking average.* [39]

Today, almost every computing technology is either running on Intel chips or has been influenced by them. It all started with Andy Grove taking ownership by first defining it and then empowering others to own it too.

Empower Team Members

Intel's Andy Grove wasn't a one-man team. He enlisted the help of the entire organization and empowered contributors to come up with the key results that would measure the objectives that they set forth.

The Intel example is a reminder of the importance of **empowering** a team to achieve the objectives centered on a clear vision. It's about driving home an emphasis of teamwork.

John Maxwell states that *"teamwork makes the dream work."* Any leader pursuing success or significance understands that this is not just some rhyme to repeat but a principle to pursue.

Any vision a leader has for the team requires the team to understand the vision; they need to buy into the vision and then be empowered to carry it out. Empowerment comes by utilizing their strengths to accomplish what needs to be done.

This idea of empowerment is further captured by a powerful thought from Melanne Verveer. *"To be a leader is to enable others to embrace a vision, initiative or assignment in a way that they feel a sense of purpose, ownership, personal engagement, and common cause."*

To achieve extreme levels of success we need others to be co-owners in the success. They need to feel as if they are part of the vision. Not to serve us, the leader, but to serve the cause we are all fighting toward, which is about *breaking average*.

Implement Solutions

Intel's marketing gambit worked because the team was tasked to come up and **implement** solutions to achieve the objectives. They also implemented a process to evaluate and measure the progress of their objectives. This process created accountability amongst the team. When you create accountability,

135

not one person wants to fall short, and ideas come forth that they are willing to implement.

As leaders, we can define the vision, cast the vision and talk about the vision. We can even empower others to pursue the vision, but at the end of the day it's about the contributors owning the vision. That means their ideas should be encouraged and considered. Look to see how their ideas might align with the vision. Be open to different options. When you see alignment of an idea with the vision, implement it. What do you have to lose? That's where big results can happen.

Implementation and execution are where many people fail. We live and work in a society with endless distractions. Most people have a bad case of SOS: Shiny Object Syndrome. This goes back to our roots. It's also one of the things that has made the world an amazing place. Our ability to come up with new ideas and explore and create new things is fascinating.

However, we need people on the team who can contribute and make things happen. Wilbur Ross says it best. *"It's important to have a sound idea, but the really important thing is the implementation."*

A Coach's Insight

WITH MIKE HARBOUR

To dig deeper, I asked Mike Harbour, who is an executive coach, and co-hosts a podcast with me on leadership, to offer some of his experiences related to the Ownership Factor. Mike is like a brother to me, and like brothers we often challenge each other. This has served to help us be better leaders and friends.

*   *   *

I grew up believing that if it is to be it is up to me. I was raised to believe this and lived it out for many years of my life. Luckily, I was introduced to some great leaders and philosophy of leadership in my early twenties and began to realize if I wanted to be a leader, I needed a team to lead. I didn't need people to do what I wanted, but I needed other leaders who were committed to the same cause.

What I have discovered is this truth, leadership truly is influence. As I learned from my experience serving in the Army, empowering the team is influence at its highest level. When a leader empowers, he/she is letting go of control, sharing the load and handing over responsibility to act in the best interest of the team.

Ownership Tips for Leaders

I've learned some amazing things can happen when you share ownership. Here are five tips that I recommend guiding you with your team:

Tip 1 - Use a Wind-Up Clock

In my life and coaching practice, I like to use a Wind-up Clock as an analogy for ownership. Why? Because to keep the wind-up clock continually ticking, I must wind it up every day. If I want the alarm to go off tomorrow, I must re-wind the clock and reset the alarm every single day.

In the same way, a *team strong leader* must have a windup clock to define the mission. Every day they need to keep the team pointed toward their true north. Every day they need to empower the team to make decisions and execute on ideas.

So, here's my challenge. Everyday set 1-3 goals for you and your team to complete or work toward. Take away the 100 things that don't matter and only focus on 1-3 big rocks. Then go do them! You'll be amazed that when you daily set your focus on what matters. It's hard not to find success.

Tip 2 - Engage the Team

Defining ownership requires the leader to engage with the team. What I recommend is to get really clear on the strengths and weaknesses of each team member. What do they add? They all offer something of value. Make sure everyone is in the right place on the team to make the biggest impact with their strengths. When you do this, you increase your overall chance of success and seeing the vision come to life.

Recognize that defining ownership is not just about the vision though, it is also about commitment. Many team members can agree that a vision is a good idea, but not all will commit to helping achieve the vision. As we shared in Chapter 5, vision must be met with values. Ownership requires everyone on the team to step one rung further up the ladder and truly commit to those values in order to achieve the vision.

Former Navy Seal and author Jocko Willink reminds us that, *"When a team takes ownership of its problems, the problem gets solved."* He emphasizes that this *"is true on the battlefield, it is true in business, and it is true in life."*

Tip 3 - Take Ultimate Responsibility

Team strong leaders understand ownership is everything. If something fails it is your fault and not someone else's. Even if someone had partial responsibility, you are ultimately responsible. This is the burden of leadership. The leader must create ownership and commitment from others and take full ownership responsibility until the end. If others see you taking on responsibility, they will do all they can to help make sure you do not fail.

Tip 4 - Involve Others in the Results

When you empower others, you don't just tell them what to do, you also involve them in the results. When you involve them in the results — even letting them refine what those key results should be — you get a whole new level of buy-in with your team and organization.

I love this quote from Tom Ridge, who was the first director of Homeland Security after the 9/11 incident. It speaks to involving others in the results. *"You have to enable and empower people to make decisions independent of you. As I've learned, each person on a team is an extension of your leadership; if they feel empowered by you, they will magnify your power to lead."* Ridge makes a powerful observation as it relates to leadership and ownership. He wants us to involve others in the result.

Tip 5 - Celebrate Small Victories

Alan Mulally, the former CEO of Ford Motor company who was instrumental in changing the culture of Ford in the past decade, shares a powerful principle. *"Leadership is having a compelling vision, a comprehensive plan, relentless implementation, and talented people working together."* [40] His thoughts echo closely with Henry Ford's — the man who pioneered *breaking average* in the automotive industry. Wasn't it Henry Ford who taught us ownership comes about by working together?

Team strong leaders execute on their requirements better than most. When you review the vision and the plan, I challenge you to also understand the strengths of each team member. In doing so, make sure you have one or two people who can implement the plan, keep the trains running on time and won't let anyone miss the mile markers along the way. What I recommend is to celebrate the small victories along the way. Every small victory gives a hunger for the next one. It's what keeps talented people working together!

Ownership Questions for Teams

The best way to get the team focused on the Ownership Factor is to ask the right questions. Here are a few questions to help evaluate and create ownership for a team. Most of these are self-reflection questions to determine if people are truly bought in.

1. Do I know who the contributors are?
2. How is each person contributing?
3. Are we committed to a common cause?
4. Do we know the goals?

5. Does each person believe in what we are doing?
6. How are we owning it?
7. How am I owning it?
8. Do our behaviors match our values?

Use these questions from time-to-time to gauge the ownership of the team. Any team member can reflect on these questions including the leader. If you as the leader find that you have a disconnect, then you need to move quickly and patch the hole. If you are a contributor and you see a problem, then take ownership of the problem by addressing it as well. Go to your team. Use candor combined with calmness. You are to be supportive not to be combative.

*   *   *

Key Takeaways

In this chapter we talked about the importance of the Ownership Factor. We explored ways to **define** ownership, **empower** contributors, and allow the team to **implement** strategies to get things done.

You can't *break average* without the Ownership Factor. Leadership expert Simon Sinek reminds us that *"A leader's job is not to do the work for others, it's to help others figure out how to do it themselves, to get things done, and to succeed beyond what they thought possible."* Sinek's perspective provides a clear emphasis on the power of ownership and *breaking average*. It's this fifth factor to *team strong leadership* that allows a team to be even more cogent and connected.

Chapter 8 - The Resilience Factor

FEATURING DAVE CORNELL

*"Only those who will risk going too far
can possibly find out how far one can go"*
— *T. S. Eliot*

The team, whatever team you are on, is going to face some battles. Yet every challenge is an opportunity for the team to be resilient and overcome those challenges. The Resilience Factor equips a team and each of its members to learn to withstand both external and internal pressures. Resilience creates **courage**. The courage to get back up when you're knocked down. The courage to persevere despite having fear or doubt.

The SimV Story

Resilience is a story that I know well. In 2000 we launched SimVentions, a software development company. The first three years of our business was full of hope but was often dashed with disappointment. We went after it with passion from the start — developing software, writing proposals, and knocking on doors.

Despite all our sweat and effort, it seemed like we couldn't get the work we wanted — and needed. Because of the struggle, we almost quit. However, just before we fully fell into the pit of despair, we realized that quitting wasn't the right move and that instead, we needed to become even more "team" focused.

Remember what we shared earlier, *"if you want to go fast, go alone, but if you want to go far go together."* By choosing to stay together, we were able to eventually see the fruits of our labor. Emphasizing team effort has always helped us find success — especially in the midst of a challenge. Why? Because a team member can always help another get back up. A team effort is the only way to stay resilient. Remember, resilience is about staying courageous.

A resilient team pours courage into each team member. That's the definition of encouragement, and it starts with the leader — you! If you don't have the courage to take the risk, then how can you expect your team to be resilient? Courage exposes the hope a leader has, and hope is vital for not just the vision, but also the team.

The team needs to see the leader's hope through the courage he or she is willing to show. In turn, they will be courageous too. The bottom line is that when you have courage, it's much easier for your team to be resilient with you. That's what we've learned in our business. If we choose to be resilient every day, we will make progress. We will find work. We will persevere. And we will bond as a team.

Right now, as I put the finishing touches on this book we are in the midst of a pandemic. For many of us, our workplace has become our home. Social distancing is the practice. There is fear and doubt. But it's time like this we can choose to come together — we can choose to stand strong. Resilience is a state of mind, and in the midst of struggle, lies our opportunity.

In this chapter, we will explore further how a leader can cultivate a resilience mindset. This includes learning how to prepare for the inevitable struggles, learning how to get back up when you get knocked down, and learning how you can support continuous improvement.

The Elements of Resilience

There are three essential elements that a leader and team must own to be resilient. They must **acknowledge** the challenges, they must **persevere** through the storms, and they must **overcome** as a team. These three elements are activators that ensure a leader and the team always stay resilient.

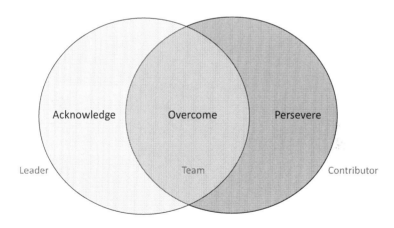

Resilience

Figure 7 – The Resilience Factor

The three elements of the Resilience Factor generate courage for the team and its members. Courage is a vital component of *breaking average*. Let's explore each of these elements and discover how the Resilience Factor can make a difference.

Acknowledge the Threats

Often the need for courage is sprung upon us when we least expect it. It's about recognizing the fears we have about those problems. When you **acknowledge** the threats, you can activate your courage, and courage leads to resilience.

All too often leaders bury their heads in the sand or wait for the "right time" to deal with a difficult challenge or issue. Courage requires us to acknowledge that we have an issue as soon as possible so that we can deal with it.

I am reminded of the famous words from the Apollo 13 mission, *"Houston, we have a problem."* [41]

Let's be real, we can't anticipate every problem, but we can acknowledge our fears about the problems. When Jim Lovell uttered those five words, *"Houston, we have a problem,"* he wasn't just acknowledging the fear, he was also identifying the need for courage. Only when we identify our need for courage can we be ready to receive the wisdom and fortitude we need to persevere. To be resilient, we must first acknowledge our fears and doubts.

My friend Dave Cornell, who travels the country and speaks on the topic of courage, shared with me a thought that hits the mark. *"Fear calls us to be spectators. Courage calls us to get in the game."* In other words, fear calls us to be average, but courage calls us to *break average*.

Listen, only when we acknowledge our fear can we put ourselves in a position to get in the game. That's the first step as a leader. The next step is to persevere.

Persevere Through the Middle

One of the most critical steps of leadership — and resilience — is to **persevere**. Perseverance is about grit and a "what-ever-it-takes" attitude. To give you a better understanding of this, I asked Dave to dig deeper and share his thoughts on perseverance. He shared with me the following story:

*   *   *

As a young boy I remember going on long car trips as a family. As we started on the road to places like the Black Hills, the west coast, or the east coast there, was always great excitement and anticipation for us as kids as we thought about all the places we would visit and the things we would see.

This enthusiasm lasted just a few hours. It didn't take long before we were tired of reading our books and playing the alphabet game or the license plate game. Soon the inevitable question would come from the back seat, *"Are We There Yet?"*

*   *   *

I had to laugh at Dave's story. We've all asked, *"Are We There Yet?"* at some point in time. It doesn't matter if you are young or old. However, when you ask it, don't you wonder if you might risk prolonging the journey even further? After all, the answer is rarely — *"Yes! We're there!"* Often, it's, *"No! Not Yet."*

As leaders, we're often asked in subtle ways, *"Are We There Yet?"* by our teams. While we would love to tell our team, *"we've arrived"*, instead we need to remind them that the journey is still ongoing. It can be long and taxing, but oh so rewarding. We need to find joy in the journey. And that joy is found in our growth, and the relationships we build along the way.

Predetermining the length of the journey, while important for deliverables and deadlines, is not always the best measure for perseverance. When we try to measure the length of the journey, it often feels like we'll never get there. It can seem to go on endlessly. Yet, it's the long journey if we stay with it that teaches us the art of perseverance in allowing us to cultivate relationships, grow in our skill, and eventually see the other side of *breaking average*. Eventually, if we persevere, we will get through!

Here's how I think of it: the longer the journey, the bigger the hill; the bigger the hill, the better the view; the better the view, the bigger the impact.

Perseverance is a leader's best friend. Perseverance doesn't quit. Perseverance creates momentum and yields success. It's what gets you to your destination — but you have to think in increments. Perseverance is the space between the starting point and the destination — it may be trying and difficult, but it's what creates opportunities.

Inevitably, at some point during this time we will hear a member of the team who is measuring for average instead of measuring for *breaking average*. They are the ones who ask, *"Are*

We There Yet?" However, the ones that are measuring for *breaking average* know it when they see it.

In her book, *Rising Strong*, Dr. Brené Brown refers to this time in our journey as the *"messy middle."* [42] This is the time when perseverance is required. It's the same resilience and courage we needed in those long car rides when we were young. If we want to experience the joy of overcoming, we must go through the *"messy middle."* We must keep our eyes focused on what our ultimate goal is. We must not turn back. We need to do whatever it takes to break through the darkness of the middle.

Any road to resilience and courage requires you to go through this stage. If you want to *break average*, you can't skip it. Think of your choices: you can either turn back and continue to live in your average world of fear and regret; or you can press on toward *breaking average*. Think of the consequences of your choice. To persevere or not to persevere? That is the question. When you put it in that context, the choice should be easy.

Reflecting on this idea of the *"messy middle"*, Dave adds the following thought to his story, *"You know. It's clear now. I would never have seen Mount Rushmore, Plymouth Rock, or the Pacific Ocean without the seemingly endless hours to get there."* Perseverance is and will always be the difference maker between an average team and a *breaking average* team. This is true of every team, whether it's a family in the car — or the founders of a company. *Team strong leadership* requires perseverance by every team member.

Overcome In the End

Perseverance, though, is not enough to be resilient. There is one more step for you and your team – one more element that is often neglected but makes all the difference. You have to finish. You have to **overcome**.

Overcome means carrying it out to completion. This means going beyond your self-perceived limitations, refusing to settle for average, and taking it as far as you can go. Overcoming is how you get through the *"messy middle."*

As you'll learn more from my friend Dave Cornell in the following section, overcoming is maintaining hope in the midst of the mess. It's about imagining standing at the finish line, looking back and saying, *"I did it!"* Then when you finally do, overcoming is about valuing all the things you've learned along the way. It's about recognizing all the people who helped you overcome. And it's about realizing you are capable of more than you gave yourself credit for.

A Coach's Insight

WITH DAVE CORNELL

The immortal words of Winston Churchill should spur us on. *"Success is not final; failure is not fatal. It is the courage to continue that counts."* Those words paint a powerful message that my friend Dave Cornell has lived first-hand. Dave and I met in Colorado at Ken Davis's SCORRE conference five years ago. That's when I learned about his story and discovered his passion for helping others be resilient. Dave is a coach, speaker and author, and I asked him if he could share more on the topic of resilience.

*   *   *

The recognition of fear in my life and the need for courage came to a head in January of 2010. That's when I lost my job. Through that whole experience I developed a new mindset of what it takes to be resilient; a mindset that I want to share with you. First, let me share with you my story.

During the middle of the recession, I went through an extended period of unemployment. A few months in, I was diagnosed with situational depression. It was during this time that I came face to face with my fears — fears I had avoided most of my life. The only way out was to become more courageous.

As I went down the long road of unemployment, I learned a very simple, but powerful lesson. In one of my darkest times I remember thinking to myself, *"I'm never going to find a job again."* That statement is pretty definitive of someone with no hope. I knew that in order for me to overcome this trying time, I had to find hope.

It was then that I noticed how a tree could grow through a rock and that weeds could come up in the cracks of a sidewalk. I realized, somehow, if those weeds and trees found a way to take root and grow in places we wouldn't expect, then so could I. That's what hope is! It's finding a crack in our despair and knowing seeds can still take root. That gave me hope to overcome.

During those days of despair, but with a vision to overcome, I learned about the power of the word "maybe." Instead of saying,

"I'm never going to find a job again," I simply added the word maybe in front of that statement, and it offered a glimmer of light to shine through. I remember saying, *"Maybe, I'm never going to find a job again — but, Maybe, I will!"*

Adding "maybe" took me from hopelessness to hopefulness. That's when I learned that overcoming is about having hope in those times where others may see none.

Resilience Tips for Leaders

I'd like to share with you a system that you can use to activate resilience for yourself as a leader as well as your team. I will share these tips by answering some of the common questions leaders facing dark times might be thinking.

Tip 1 - Ask the Fear Question

This first question is essential to overcoming your fears that limit you in being resilient as a leader.

How should we acknowledge our fear and identify the courage we need?

There are two ways.

1. **Write your fear down or verbally share it with someone you trust**. In many ways, fear can be similar to an alcohol or drug addiction. Until we are willing to admit we have the issue we will never deal with it. Avoidance is a common way of dealing with our fears. Writing them down or sharing them with someone is the first step to overcoming your fear.

2. **Recognize your "self-talk."** We must be aware of what is going on in our mind to face our fears successfully. If you want to start your own business but, in your mind, you say to yourself, *"I want to start and run my own business, but I don't think I have the skills to do so,"* you are probably correct. The negative mindset is one of the symptoms of fear in our lives. Be aware of what you say in your mind so you can change the "self-talk" when you hear it.

Tip 2 - Ask the Fight Question

This second question is powerful in helping you get clarity on what action to take in response to fear.

How do we fight on and gain the resolve to persevere?

Begin to see your fears through a different lens. When fear affects us in our daily lives, we think it is only impacting us and no one else. The reality is our fears impact not only our lives but the lives of those around us. It could be our family, our employees, our customers or many others.

If, as an employer, you were afraid to hold an employee accountable for their actions, would you be the only one impacted by that? No, of course not. The employee would be impacted because they wouldn't have the opportunity to grow and learn. Other employees would be affected because they would wonder why this employee is able to get away with their actions. This wondering of other employees will affect your company as trust decreases. From there, the effect compounds until it reaches countless people you wouldn't even expect it to.

You need to see these kinds of irrational fears as selfish. Not courageously facing these fears is self-protection. This self-protection, however, comes at the expense of others. Ask yourself this question: who is paying a price for your fear?

Tip 3 - Ask the Action Question

Courage is about action. Courage is about taking steps without knowing the outcome. This next question is powerful in helping us take action.

How do we overcome and reach our goals or dreams?

In order to overcome your fear, you need to take the first step. People avoid the first step because they are afraid to fail. They want to wait until the fear is gone before moving ahead. The first step is recognizing the fear will always be there. Don't wait for it to go away or you will never take your first step. The old movie cowboy John Wayne once said, *"Courage is being scared to death but saddling up anyway!"*

Rather than thinking about all the steps you have to take, focus on the one step you can take today to move in the right direction? Take that step and then think about the next step. When we went on those long car rides as children, we didn't complete the trip in one day. The long journey was broken up into shorter journeys. What action will you take today to get you closer to your dream?

Resilience Questions for Teams

One of the best ways to motivate the team to stay resilient is to offer them questions that they can use to elevate awareness and encourage each other. Take a moment to consider the following questions to help you engage with your team, and for them to engage with one another.

1. What challenges are in front of us?
2. What have we been afraid to acknowledge? Why?
3. What is your fear about facing these challenges?
4. What might happen if we don't courageously take on our fears and apprehension?
5. How can we begin to see our fears differently?
6. Who is paying a price because of these fears?
7. What is one step you can take today to begin to face your challenge(s)?

*   *   *

Key Takeaways

In this chapter we talked about the importance of the Resilience Factor. Resilience is a sign of a great team and a great leader. Challenges will come to every team. It's not that we won't fail, it's whether or not we get back up. As *team strong leaders*, we have the opportunity to create teams that are resilient. It starts with **acknowledging** the obstacles. It's followed by a steadfastness in **persevering** among *team strong contributors*, and finally it requires a team that believes they will **overcome** any challenge.

You can't *break average* without also having resilience. Ralph Waldo Emerson said it best. *"The greatest glory in living lies not in never falling, but in rising every time we fall."* The good news is that as *team strong leaders*, we can inject the hope — the fortitude — to help our teams rise when they fail.

In closing, Sheryl Sandberg, who is the author and chief operating officer (COO) at Facebook reminds us, *"there are things that we can all do to build resilience in ourselves, but also to build resilience in each other."* She is emphasizing how resilience is a *me to we* quality. This is why resilience, the sixth factor to *team strong leadership*, must be sought after in our pursuit of *breaking average*.

Chapter 9 - The Yes Factor

FEATURING TRUDY MENKE

"It's determination and commitment to an unrelenting pursuit of your goal — a commitment to excellence — that will enable you to attain the success you seek."
— *Mario Andretti*

Contrary to what you might think, the Yes Factor is not about always saying *"yes"* to everything. It's about saying *"yes"* to one thing, and that one thing is being laser-focused on a vision to *break average*.

Breaking average requires commitment from everyone on the team, starting with the leader. You can't have a mix of *"yeses"* and *"nos."* That just won't work. Yes, creates **commitment**; a commitment to move ahead and a commitment to excellence.

Commitment starts with the leader saying *"yes"*. Yes, to the possibilities, and the ideas that are centered on the vision. That then creates alignment among others who say *"yes."* Finally, it's about the team believing that *"yes, we will find a way to reach the vision."*

The Greatest Showman

There is no better story that reflects the Yes Factor — and *breaking average* — then the making of the movie *The Greatest Showman*, starring Hugh Jackman. This larger-than-life musical about P.T. Barnum and his famous circus of entertainers, is a fun watch and inspiring movie. [43] What's equally inspiring is the story of how the movie was made.

The inspiration for the movie, of course, is the extraordinary life story of P.T. Barnum, who lived a century and a half ago. Barnum had a vision to entertain people in ways they had never seen before. His dreams were lofty and were considered by many as far-fetched, but he had a vision. Despite his rough-around-the-edges personality, he pursued and succeeded in *breaking average* in a big way.

One of the ways he deviated from average, was how he offered hope to social outcasts with raw talent by giving them an opportunity to be part of his vision. He gave them a sense of belonging. This element of teamwork is reflected well in the movie.

Despite the crazy dreams that Barnum had, and the challenges he faced, he found ways for others to say *"yes"*. Again, what's fascinating isn't just Barnum's story, it's the backstory for the creation of the movie about his life.

From concept to creation it took seven-years of fighting to make the movie. Each step of the arduous process was about finding ways for others to say *"yes"*. One of the first and instrumental *"yeses"* was getting a commitment from the legendary actor Hugh Jackman early on to take the lead role. The next challenge was composing a musical score, then gaining funding commitments, and then, of course, to filling out of the cast with the right talent and actors, some of whom had never sung in a movie before. It was working to get one *"yes"* after another.

It would have been easy for many people to just say *"no"* and give up. However, the director, Michael Gracey, and the leading actor, Hugh Jackman, chose to lead with a Yes Factor mindset. This choice created a ripple effect. Soon, one by one, the actors, song writers, entertainers, and choreographers said *"yes"*, and it all came together into something amazing.

During production in between sets, Jackman was caught on film commenting, *"It is so sweet — so sweet — I'm enjoying every entire bit."* His comment serves as a reminder that one of the great benefits of the Yes Factor is the satisfaction that a team unilaterally feels the benefits together.

If there wasn't a commitment to *"yes"*, then the world would have missed out on a mesmerizing story. P.T. Barnum himself once shared some powerful words that help set the frame for the Yes Factor. *"Whatever you do, do it with all your might. Work at it, early and late, in season and out of season, not leaving a stone unturned, and never deferring for a single hour that which can be done just as well now."*

As can be observed in the making of a movie, or the journey of any project, establishing a *"yes"* mindset requires commitment from all parties. Without commitment you don't have a leader, you don't have contributors, and you don't have a dream. Commitment is the shared responsibility that leaders and contributors make together, which unite them as a team.

The Elements of the *"Yes Factor"*

There are three essential elements of a well led team that reflect the Yes Factor. Commitment doesn't just happen by itself. It happens because we feel invited as leaders to participate and we feel led to **invite** others to join us. When we do that, we see contributors who **align** themselves to the cause. Then, and only then, can we see a team that **believes** in the possibility — the hope — of what can be. This is tied to a vision and a mission that the team pursues.

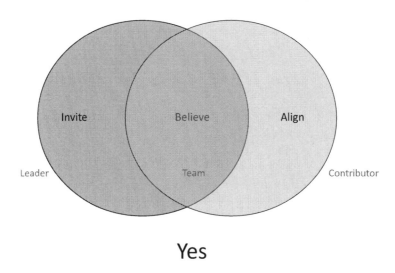

Yes

Figure 8 – The Yes Factor

The three elements of the Yes Factor serve as activators that influence healthy commitment by the team. Let's explore each of these elements further.

Invite Your Team

Leaders lead because they feel a sense of **invitation**. They feel called. Great leaders extend their calling by inviting others to join the cause. This is important. The invite signals belief. First leaders must believe in themselves to lead the vision, and secondly, leaders must authentically believe in others.

They have a sense that they have been invited into something bigger than themselves, and that the invitation isn't just for them.

What's required for this belief to take hold and to manifest itself is charisma. Charisma is like fuel to a fire of a leader's vision. It helps create "buy-in" and "commitment". Charisma can increase the speed of the *"yes"*. As a leader, your Yes Factor level directly maps with your charisma.

Charisma has little to do with your personality trait, but more to do with the appeal you have as a leader. Charisma is about showing up; it's about being willing to connect with those around you. It's about having and showing interest at a personal level.

As the leading actor and advocate for the film, *The Greatest Showman,* Hugh Jackman provided charisma in spades, both on film and in-between sets.

Listen to this incredible account of what Jackman did to influence a core group of investors who flew into New York to determine if they were going to financially support *The Greatest Showman* movie project.

The day before the big event, Jackman had an emergency nasal surgery. The surgeon wouldn't let Jackman leave the hospital unless he promised not to sing the next day. His concern was that if Jackman sang, he would open his stitches.

Rather than cancel the event, Hugh Jackman and director Michael Gracey simply pivoted on what they were going to do. They brought in a well-known Broadway actor, Jeremy Jordan, to shadow Jackman on the stage and sing Jackman's parts while Jackman mined the key scenes. [44]

It was going well, but Jackman sensed it wasn't convincing enough to the potential investors. Jackman's charisma wouldn't let him stay silent any longer. The actor best known for his other bold and dynamic roles, such as Wolverine, needed to persuade the investors that he had the voice — not just the face and acting skills — to play the lead role. His intuition saw an invitation to say *"yes",* so he relieved Jordan for the final song and took center stage and began singing one of the movie's more powerful ballads, *From Now On.*

What happened next blew everyone away. Michael Gracey, the director, recalls the moment, *"Everyone jumped up on top of their seats."* The charisma began being echoed by the investors creating the *"yes"* that was needed. Gracey added, *"It was a euphoric moment. The man that everyone had come to hear sing was finally singing. That's when we got the greenlight!"*

Where does charisma like this come from? Years earlier, actor Patrick Stewart, who played Professor Charles Xavier in the X-Men movies, recalls meeting Jackman for the very first time when he was a late addition to play Wolverine in the first movie. His account might reveal just where this type of charisma comes from.

"We'd been shooting for a week or maybe more, and we were running out of stuff to shoot without someone to play Logan.

One morning this slender, pleasant-looking guy with a strong Australian accent is introduced to us all. He spent 15 to 20 minutes chatting, and by the time he was called to do his reading, we'd fallen in love. He charmed everybody."

The tip off words from Stewart was that he *"charmed everybody."* Those two words reflect the heart of a charismatic leader. It's about someone who genuinely cares and isn't afraid to show it. It doesn't matter their personality, what matters is if their heart is into it. If your heart's into it, the invitations will come, and you will be able to invite others to join you in your vision.

Align Their Values

What occurs after an invitation is something powerful — something we call **alignment**. Consider the inspirational story of actress and singer Keala Settle.

Keala auditioned for the part of the singing bearded lady in *The Greatest Showman*. She shares, *"I just thought I was coming in for two different presentations and that would be it."*

Let me pause for a moment. Based on her comments, she never thought she would get the part, but she went for it anyhow. That's a factor of resilience. Facing our fear by still saying *"yes"*, gives us the courage to *break average*. By saying *"yes"* she competed and performed for the role. And in spite of her doubt, she got it!

When we show a commitment to yes — when we align ourselves with a vision — good things can happen. Little did Keala realize how much of an impact she would make with her performance.

Her song in the movie is not only powerful to moviegoers, it resonated deeply with the cast when they performed it. Everyone on the team became aligned to it.

Check out some of the words.

> *When the sharpest words*
> *wanna cut me down*
> *I'm gonna send a flood,*
> *gonna drown them out*
> *I am brave, I am bruised*
> *I am who I'm meant to be, this is me.*
> *Look out, cause here I come*
> *And I'm marching on to the beat I drum*
> *I'm not scared to be seen*
> *I make no apologies, this is me!*

The song reminds us that we must live *all out*; regardless of the walls we face. Life provides each of us the opportunity to be brave, and to lean more completely into who we are meant to be. It truly is about living the Yes Factor and having others around us live it out too! It's about alignment, and alignment is what makes a team unstoppable.

How does alignment happen? It's simple, but profound. Contributors align when their values are reflected in the vision the leader invites them to join. When they align with the leader, when they align their purpose, then they align as a team.

The song, by the way, is a reminder that while others may tell us *"no"*, it's still ultimately our choice. We can say *"yes"* and align ourselves to *breaking average.*

Believe The Vision

Once you **invite** others and you begin to see contributors **align**, the third element of **believe**, will flourish. The noun form of believe is the word "belief". Belief is the attitude that something is pure, noble and true. When a team has belief — when they believe — you can see it. It's the type of attitude that spreads to others. An attitude of belief is a choice. The contributors on a team choose to believe. Belief speaks to the momentum the team can experience as it relates to the Yes Factor.

A lack of shared belief exposes the cracks and causes division. It can cause defeat. However, shared belief is infectious and helps fill the gaps and create confidence for a team. Belief turns impossible dreams into possibilities.

Michael Gracey, the director of *The Greatest Showman* shares that the one thing he will always remember is *"the people who signed up for that impossible dream. Who believed in it and brought it to life."* [45] Belief is a powerful force. Belief is contagious.

Nothing is impossible as long as the team believes. It starts with the leader's invitation. It's followed by the team's alignment. And when the leaders and contributors unite it fuels and expands their belief.

A Coach's Insight

WITH TRUDY MENKE

To dive deeper on the topic of the Yes Factor, I asked my friend and business coach Trudy Menke to share some of her experiences and insights. Trudy has a clear understanding and appreciation of the value that different personas have on a team. She speaks life into leaders helping them in the areas of communication and commitment.

*   *   *

As a trainer and executive coach, I enjoy the opportunity to look at leadership through the lens of different businesses, industries, and nonprofits. I especially enjoy looking for patterns in leadership and communication that pertain to all of them.

Usually I'm coming alongside the leaders as a thinking partner and asking questions that they think through from a 30,000-foot perspective. I'm often reminding them to lift their thinking higher, often beyond the day-to-day, and to learn more firmly into their leadership roles.

Recently I was challenged to get out of my own comfort zone — not as a leader, but as a team member on an international mission trip that I never expected to make. The experience was eye opening, especially as it relates to the Yes Factor.

The Invitation

Rachel Werner, the director of U.S. operations for the Hippo Valley Christian Mission is a friend of mine. She and I have known each other for 20 years. Our paths cross occasionally, and recently she asked me to join her on a mission trip to Zimbabwe. [46]

Little did I know then how I would see the elements of *invite*, *align* and *believe* come together to create an amazing *"yes"* experience for all. Rachel has been on many mission trips, including four trips to Zimbabwe. Her invitation started me on the journey to *"yes"*.

Here's one thing that I noticed. When an invite is delivered, the person doing the inviting automatically assumes a leadership role in the eyes of the person being invited. Additionally, the invite immediately signals two things:

1. It signals the leader's belief in the vision (in this case, the mission trip and the organization behind it), and
2. It signals the leader's belief in the person she is inviting. For instance, I felt certain Rachel wouldn't have invited me if she didn't think I could add value to the vision.

The Alignment

Part of the conversation that followed Rachel's initial Invite included sharing with me how I would add value to the vision. The mission trip included trips to schools and an orphanage, but it also included a conference for teachers and chaplains with a goal to add strong leadership content. That's the part that resonated with me.

Rachel was deepening the invitation by helping me see where I could Align with the vision. I already knew her well enough to know I was aligned with her as a leader and person, but now I was aligning with the vision she was proposing.

I asked questions and created alternative solutions to her vision that wouldn't include me. (That was fear and a lack of self-assurance talking.) Her competence and confidence helped me to align more completely and ultimately accept her offer.

Key to the conversation was when I recognized that two of my values and priorities (teaching leadership and communication and promoting a strong faith life) would be fulfilled throughout the trip as we interacted with children, teachers and chaplains. Once I realized this key alignment, I was all in! That's what alignment does.

The Belief

After the leader Invites and followers align, there's a coming together of shared belief. Belief in the vision, belief in the mission, and a belief in one another.

How does shared belief happen? Well, both the leader and the contributor understand their roles, they see how they fit. It's the merger of these parts and pieces that create the *"yes"* — and the *"yes"* isn't quiet. It's an emotional exclamation—*"Yes!"*

Once the leader and contributors start to create this momentum in their relationship, there's a great likelihood that the project and the work will gain momentum too. When you see this process taking shape with a vision, then you are witnessing a mark of *team strong leadership.*

"Yes" Tips for Leaders

I have a few tips I'd like to share to help you lead others to *"yes"*. I encourage you to take time to put these in practice.

Tip 1 - Invite Others

When you go from informing people to inviting people, the vision becomes more relational, especially when the invitation is delivered in person. Relying on any other way to market or advertise an invitation will often fall short. As a. leader, be sure to make your invitation relational and intentional.

To understand this truth, think back to your favorite teacher. Imagine for a moment, this leader in your younger life, putting a big box of crayons on a table in the middle of the room. Wouldn't that be an invitation to open the box? Wouldn't that be a table where you would want to sit?

As a leader, when you invite others to sit at the round table, you want to connect your vision with their individual needs and dreams — with the stories and pictures in their mind. Therefore, your invitation must create intrigue.

Here are some suggestions to make sure you are casting an invitation that grabs the attention of others.

- Does your invitation express a belief in an idea centered on a problem that needs to be solved?
- Does your invitation offer clarity of how others fit in to make it happen?

- Do you provide contributors some options on how they can contribute? (Metaphorically, using our classroom example, can they choose which crayon they want to use to add color to the project?)
- Do you make it easy for them to get started? (You want to make it easy for them to open their big box of crayons and say *"yes."*

These questions will help ensure you are offering something of value that others will want to commit to.

Tip 2 - Create Alignment

Alignment comes when there's clarity of values and priorities. If the values and priorities of those you are inviting match with the invitation of the vision, then alignment is possible.

As a leader, take time to understand the values and priorities of your contributors. Help ensure that those values and priorities will be satisfied. If their values and priorities aren't in harmony with yours, then it may be best to let them pursue something else and let them go. You don't want to force the alignment, for someone who isn't on the same page. That could lead to a limited belief that postpones or eliminates a true *"yes."*

Tip 3 - Establish Belief

Alignment, once you are able to get it, isn't enough though. The next step is for your team to have a strong belief in the vision and each other.

How can you develop and deepen a *"yes"* belief? The first step is understanding that not every contributor on a team who says, *"Yes, I believe!"* are saying the same thing.

Let's step back a moment. Knowing where a *"yes"* can be strongest with a team member is tied to understanding how their values align with the invitation. Their values expose their why. For belief to take hold, people need to be motivated by their alignment of their values to the vision, but it also can be enhanced by their alignment to the leader or members of the team. Without alignment in both, there is no belief.

To become the best leader for every individual on a team, go back and look for mutual agreement. Here are some suggested attributes to evaluate along with questions to ask yourself to ensure alignment.

Table 4 – The Alignment Evaluation Map

Attribute	Alignment Questions
Character	Can they commit to working with you? Do they show belief in your character? Do they value your integrity, knowledge and past achievements?
Vision	Can they commit to working toward your vision? Does it mean something to them?
People	Can they commit to working on this particular team? Do they believe in, like, and value the people who are also contributing?

Purpose	Can they commit to working on this vision, because they believe it fits with their life purpose or core values?
Growth	Can they commit to working with leadership? Do they believe that they will grow personally and professionally under their influence?
Dream	Can they commit to working on the dream? Do they believe it will make a difference in the world?

One more thing. As a leader, are you willing to set aside your personal alignment to the vision and let your contributors explore their own? Are you willing to put aside your *"yes"* to help the team members find their *"yes"*?

To do this, you will need to think of them individually and allow your vision to serve them first before they join you. It means letting them take their favorite crayons out of the big box and letting them know for sure that *"yes"*, you value those colors too, and you trust how they will be expressed in their hands. When you do this well, your team members will follow you anywhere.

"Yes" Team Questions

The best way to get the team focused on the Yes Factor is to ask clear questions. Take a moment to consider the following questions that team members can be asked to validate their *"yes"*.

1. Has the dream or vision been explained with sound logic and compelling emotion?
2. Why did you say *"yes"*? What did you hope to gain?

3. Why did other members on the team say "yes"? Which reasons were most important to you? What did they hope to gain?

4. What types of behaviors or agreements are essential to preserve the *"yes"* for you? For the team?

5. What would make a *"yes"* turn to a *"no?"* What process should we create to check and balance that?

These are powerful questions, but you want to make sure the team has been established first. These are tough questions to answer. If you ask these questions to an uncommitted team who haven't yet officially claimed their seat at the table, it might only further separate them. However, if you ask these questions to them once they've taken their seat, it will energize them to stay seated and work together. When we experience a collective *"yes"*, it encourages us and unites us.

An example of this is the power of a simple Facebook group for an individual who may have just signed up for a new program. At first, their *"yes"* was strong, but the good intent will wane unless it's cultivated immediately. A Facebook group where others have also said *"yes"* and are active will encourage them and excite them.

*   *   *

Key Takeaways

In this chapter we talked about the importance of the Yes Factor. The Yes Factor is about commitment. Commitment requires you to be bold as a *team strong leader* and cast a big vision by **inviting** *team strong contributors* to join you. Commitment requires contributors who are **aligned** with the vision and who can take direction. Finally, commitment allows a team to come together and **believe** together. It is only when we pull together as a team, that we can seize on opportunities and deliver on a big dream.

After the 1936 U.S. Olympic Rowing team won the gold medal, all nine team members vowed to stay connected and gather at least yearly to commemorate their victory with a good old fashion row. Every 10 years they would return to the boathouse where it all started at the University of Washington. They would pull their old shell out of the boathouse, carry her down to the dock, and paddle her down Lake Washington. They did this for five decades straight, all the way up until 1986 — fifty years after their victory in Germany. It's an example of how the Yes Factor never really dies.

Until their health began to fail them, they always embraced the invitation. They craved alignment. And they reminisced on what they believed from decades earlier. They never forgot the power of *breaking average*.

It wasn't uncommon to also see others come out and greet these legends. It wasn't an exclusive club; it was an open invitation. Many would fantasize what it must have been like to beat the likes of Hitler's elite as these Olympic legends glided their shell through the water. It wasn't uncommon to see someone trying to take pictures or hoping to bump into one of them and introduce themselves. They would shake their hand and thank them. For those watching it also created alignment, and, since we can continue to tell the story, it still ignites belief. That's because the Yes Factor is contagious.

Truth be told you can't *break average* without the Yes Factor — without commitment. John Maxwell shares that, *"If you want to be an effective leader, you have to be committed. True commitment inspires and attracts people. It shows them that you have conviction. They will believe in you only if you believe in your cause."*

Commitment is centered on *"yes"*. This is why the Yes Factor, which is the seventh factor of *team strong leadership*, is an important arc to *breaking average*.

Chapter 10 - How VICTORY is Possible

*"Victory is always possible for the person who
refuses to stop fighting."*
— *Napoleon Hill*

Let's face it, there are times where things look grim. Times where the journey toward the vision seems impossible, and all we feel are the headwinds, or the crisis around us.

How refreshing is it to know *"victory is always possible for the person [and the team] who refuses to stop fighting."* These words from Napoleon Hill offer hope.

Think back on the 1936 U.S. Olympic rowing team. They found a way to stay in the fight, despite the challenges around them. Think also about the Wright Brothers and Katherine Wright, Walt Disney, Jackie Robinson,. None of them could have accomplished what they did without a team. Victory is always possible for the team that keeps going.

Choose the Infinite Game

The desire for *breaking average* is what unites a team. It's what results in *team strong leadership.* The key thing to watch out for though is finite game thinking.

Finite game thinking believes there is a finish line. Finite game thinking measures for average. It happens when we compare our present condition to what we have done in the past rather than the vision for what we have in the future.

With finite game thinking, achieving any success tempts us to fall prey to *Destination Disease*, which Jay shared about earlier in Chapter 6. This is the belief that once you and your team achieve a goal, you can claim success. But it doesn't quite work that way.

What we need to do instead is to continually measure for VICTORY. This is what we call "infinite game thinking." As Simon Sinek puts it. *"There is no finish line."* We need to continue to play an infinite game — a game that doesn't end, and a game that never settles for average. [47]

Settling for average — finite game thinking — is a dream killer. Look at any business that experienced remarkable success early on, got comfortable and stagnated because of that success, they settled for average. Think of Borders, Kodak, Circuit City, Blockbusters, Radio Shack and others.

Do you want to know why these businesses died?

Each of them fell victim to *Destination Disease*. It turns out that once you have success, there is an insatiable temptation to protect what you have. Instead of keeping the foot on the gas of innovation, it's easy to get distracted by the light of success. We can begin to brake and start rubbernecking — rewatching what we have accomplished and relishing in how we did it. How easy is to forget that, *"Pride goeth before a fall?"* [48]

Business rubbernecking can happen when too much focus is put on comparing quarterly performance to past numbers. It's also referred to as financial rubbernecking, which is compounded when we begin to compare ourselves to others playing their own finite games. When your goal becomes to meet or beat the numbers and sustain your success, watch out! You may be tempted to take your foot off the gas. You may be rubbernecking.

To avoid *Destination Disease*, keep your eye on the vision. Turn to infinite game thinking. The vision must always be something ahead not behind. Innovation is always about disruption, not comfort. With finite game thinking, success might tempt you to slow down and stop innovating, but don't! Keep disrupting. It is better to fail and get back up, then to succeed and sit down.

Finite game thinking will also cause you to look at the here and now. If there is a crisis, it could paralyze you. But infinite game thinking looks for solutions and sees the opportunity in the midst of a challenge. Think of the great teams that endure the struggles and still make a difference. Here are a few: The Walt Disney Company, Walgreens, Apple, Ford Motor Company, and Southwest Airlines. Are these companies perfect? No! But they all have endured and continue to add value.

We can't find VICTORY and maintain VICTORY unless we continually push past average. If we compare ourselves to average, then we are always measuring ourselves to the past — falling prey to finite game thinking.

Measure for VICTORY

Instead of using average as a means to evaluate a team, use the VICTORY Framework instead. Average is a measure of the past, whereas the VICTORY Framework is a measure of the future.

Here's how to assess yourself and your team. We encourage you to use the TSL Scorecard in Appendix B to capture your ratings.

VISION - Assess the Clarity

The first factor is **vision**. To evaluate vision, you assess its clarity. Clarity is what gives leadership and the team focus. You can identify clarity by evaluating the three elements of vision: the **dream**, the **declaration**, and the **delivery**. Here are some questions for you to consider.

1. How has leadership dared to *dream*?
2. What are team members doing to *declare* the dream?
3. What is the team doing to *deliver* the dream?

INSIGHT - Assess the Comprehension

Vision is only the beginning to unlocking the power of the VICTORY Framework. Another is **insight**, which gives a leader and the team greater focus. For insight you want to assess the comprehension. Comprehension reflects our degree of understanding, as well as what the leader and the team are doing to be proactive in sourcing wisdom and gathering intel. You can identify comprehension by evaluating the three elements of insight: **foresight**, **hindsight**, and **engage-sight.** Here are some questions for you to consider.

1. How is leadership seeking *foresight*?
2. What are team members doing to share *hindsight*?
3. What is the team doing to offer *engage-sight*?

COLLABORATION - Assess the Chemistry

Collaboration is a key component to *team strong leadership,* but it may be the most neglected. People are often afraid to get out of their bubble and make an impact, but collaboration is all about making collisions. For collaboration you want to assess team chemistry. You can identify chemistry by evaluating the three elements of collaboration: **communication**, **co-operation**, and **interaction**. Here are some questions for you to consider.

1. How is leadership working to *communicate*?
2. What are team members doing to *co-operate*?
3. What is the team doing to *interact*?

TRUST - Assess the Confidence

The one piece of the VICTORY Framework that will make or break a team the fastest is **trust**. Trust is what creates confidence with one another. For trust, you want to assess the confidence in several relationships: Leader to Leader, Leader to Contributors, Contributors to Leader, and Contributors to Contributors. How confident is the team? You identify confidence by evaluating the elements of trust: **credibility**, **dependability**, and **serviceability**. Here are some questions to help guide you.

1. How is leadership staying *credible*?
2. What are team members doing to be *dependable*?
3. What is the team doing to *serve*?

OWNERSHIP - Assess the Connections

For **ownership** you want to assess the connections that are taking root. Connection gives individuals on the team a sense of belonging. You can identify connections by evaluating the three elements of ownership: the **defined** opportunities, the degree of **empowerment**, and the resulting **implementation**. Here are some questions for you to consider.

1. How is leadership *defining* opportunities?
2. What are team members *empowered* to do?
3. What is the team doing to *implement* ideas?

RESILIENCE - Assess the Courage

Breaking average teams don't fold under pressure because they practice the Resilience Factor. Resilience complements all the other factors in the VICTORY Framework. For resilience you want to assess the courage of the team. Courage is what grants permission to the leadership and team to forge ahead despite any fear, doubt, or challenge. You can identify courage by evaluating the three elements of resilience: **acknowledgment**, **perseverance**, and **overcoming**. Here are some questions for you to consider.

1. How is leadership *acknowledging* the threats?
2. What are team members' level of *perseverance*?
3. What is the team doing to show they are *overcomers*?

YES - Assess the Commitment

The final key to unlocking VICTORY is the power of **yes**. For the Yes Factor, you want to assess the team's commitment to one another. Commitment reflects the "all-in" mentality of a team and its members and is critical to *breaking average*. You can identify it by evaluating the three elements of yes: the **invitation**, the **alignment**, and the **belief**. Here are some questions for you to consider.

1. How is leadership offering **invites**?
2. What are team members doing to **align** with the plan?
3. What is the team doing to show they **believe** in the cause?

Why Breaking Average Matters

What matters more than simply following the VICTORY Framework, is to remember the *why* behind it. Why does *breaking average* and *team strong leadership* matter? It matters because we're meant to add value to others. If we don't *break average*, we won't make the impact that we could and should. Being unified as a team is the most powerful way to add that value. In fact, value is multiplied with a team.

We want to leave with you three simple but powerful precepts. They are patterns of leadership that will influence your thinking and help you live your *why*.

- True leaders never lead alone
- Standout teams play the infinite game
- Great teams always need a guide

We recommend putting these precepts on a note card near your desk or computer — somewhere you spend a lot of time. Be reminded of them daily and understand what each one truly means.

1. True Leaders Never Lead Alone

Observation has proven that the best leaders are the ones that have the best teams, and the best teams have the best leaders. In other words, you can't have one without the other.

When leaders and teams work together, they become a tightly knit group that nurtures other leaders. They are the ones that *break average* and reaching uncommon results. The starting point is understanding this precept — true leaders never lead alone.

2. Standout Teams Play the Infinite Game

How do you know if the team you are leading has the right mindset? Simon Sinek makes an acute observation. *"Players with an infinite mindset want to leave their organizations in better shape than they found them."* [49] When you see this behavior, then you know you have a team ready to *break average*.

3. Great Teams Always Need a Guide

Great teams are never great at the start. It takes work. Teams need others who are willing to pursue the dream with them. Teams discover that in order to go where they need to go — to fully live their purpose and achieve their potential — they need someone to guide them. They need leaders. They need you!

Every winning team has discovered that they needed to be effectively led to be successful. They need someone who mentors them and guides them. They need a leader who *"knows the way, goes the way, and shows the way."* [50] These are the type of leaders who influence a team in the cause of *breaking average*.

The Final Secret — *"Be the Guide"*

What if you allowed yourself to see every team member as a hero, and you as their guide? [51] How different might your team or organization be?

The heroes you are serving are the members on your team – fellow leaders and contributors. However, with the challenges they face, they may not know they are the heroes. As a leader, your opportunity is to be the guide who can offer these heroes a plan. It's not about you, it's about them. Your success comes by being a blessing to others as the guide.

Think back to Coach Al Ulbrickson, described in Chapter 1. He was the guide for nine young men who persevered to Olympic glory. He didn't need to get in the boat with the team, he just needed to guide them to the vision of *breaking average*!

Think back also to Katharine Wright described in Chapter 2. She was the guide for her brothers Wilbur and Orville. As smart as Wilbur and Orville may have been, she was the only family member with a college education — she was a teacher with empathy. As a teacher, the guide doesn't need to know all the answers, they just need to encourage those in their care to find the answers for themselves, and that's what Katharine did! She encouraged her brothers, the heroes.

Almost every core leader mentioned in this book served as a guide who encouraged others with values and vision. This includes Andy Groves, John F. Kennedy, Walt Disney, Branch Rickey, Al

Harrison, and even Steve Jobs. The real heroes were the members of the teams that they served and guided.

The guide knows this, settling for average is what limits a team's ability. "Average" causes individuals and teams to be less than their best. The guide knows that potential isn't in "average." True potential can only be found by *breaking average*. The VICTORY mindset, therefore, is how *team strong leaders* and *team strong contributors* work together to discover bold new ways of *breaking average*!

*   *   *

One last thing. It turns out that every guide needs a plan. May this book serve as that plan for you? To further equip you, we leave with you the VICTORY Mindset Manifesto on the next page. Let it serve as a reminder of the important things you can do to be a *team strong leader*.

The VICTORY Mindset Manifesto

VICTORY is always possible
for the team that stays focused
on the mindset of breaking average!
It starts with each of us.

Share with the team your Vision,
Gather from others their Insight,
Work to always Collaborate,
Transfer to others Trust,
Create a sense of Ownership,
Choose to demonstrate Resilience,
And give others a reason to say "Yes!"

These are the factors that allow
common people to attain uncommon results.
It is the picture of team strong leadership.

Appendix A - Quick Guide

The following table offers a quick view of each *team strong leadership* factor, including tips for leaders, and questions for teams.

Table 5 – VICTORY Framework Quick Guide

Factor	Tips for Leaders	Questions for Teams
The Vision Factor Goal = CLARITY Elements: • Dream It • Declare It • Deliver It	• Start with Authentic Journaling • Reflect on "I Have a Dream…" • Capture "I am" Affirmation Statements • Take Time to Check-In	• Who do you want to be? • What do you care about? • Why does your vision matter? • How do we make it a lasting vision? • How do we continue to create buy-in?
The Insight Factor Goal = COMPREHENSION Elements: • Foresight • Hindsight • Engage-sight	• Observe the Needs • Evaluate the Experience • Ride the Wave • Confront the Truth	• What are the needs? • Who is it for? • What do you like? • What do you wish was different? • How can we do it better?
The Collaboration Factor Goal = CHEMISTRY Elements:	• Ask the Right Questions • Take Time to Listen • Keep up the Tempo • Learn to Laugh Together	• What is our Definition of Done? • What's our Work Backlog? • What's our Sprint Backlog?

• Communicate • Co-operate • Interact		• What's our MVP? • Who's Got What? • How is it Going -- seriously?
The Trust Factor Goal = CONFIDENCE Elements: • Be Credible • Be Dependable • Be Serving	• Give Trust to Earn Trust • Evaluate Trust Levels • Start Small • Make It Safe • Know Your Strengths • Give Permission to Challenge • Make it Repeatable • Stay Accountable • Serve Them Like Braveheart! • Compound the Interest	• Do you mind if I get your viewpoint? • What is your opinion? • What do you think are our strengths? • What do you think are the opportunities? • Would you mind helping me out? • What would you do? • What am I missing? • What do you recognize as the strengths each contributor brings?
The Ownership Factor Goal = CONNECTION Elements: • Define • Empower • Implement	• Use a Wind-Up Clock • Engage the Team • Take Ultimate Responsibility • Involve Others in the Results • Celebrate Small Victories	• Do I know who the contributors are? • How is each person contributing? • Are we committed to a common cause? • Do we know the goals? • Does each person believe in what we are doing? • How are we owning it? • How am I owning it?

		• Do our behaviors match our values?
The Resilience Factor Goal = COURAGE Elements: • Acknowledge • Persevere • Overcome	• Ask the Fear Question • Ask the Fight Question • Ask the Action Question	• What challenges are in front of us? • What have we been afraid to acknowledge? Why? • What is your fear about facing these challenges? • What might happen if you don't courageously take on our fears and apprehension? • How can we begin to see our fears differently? • Who is paying the price because of these fears? • What is one step you can take today to begin to face your challenge(s)?
The Yes Factor Goal = COMMITMENT Elements: • Invite • Align • Believe	• Invite Others • Create Alignment • Establish Belief	• Has the dream or vision been explained with sound logic and compelling emotion? • Why did you say Yes? What did you hope to gain? • Why did other members on the team say Yes? Which

		reasons were most important to you? • What types of behaviors or agreements are essential to preserve our Yes for you? For the team? • What would make a Yes turn to a No? What process should we create to check and balance that?

Appendix B - The TSL Scorecard

Chapter 10 provided insight on how to evaluate *team strong leadership* (TSL) by using the VICTORY Framework as a measure. We also wanted to provide an easy to use team scorecard to help you capture and grade the factors and actors.

Table 6 – The TSL Scorecard

Factors	Actors			TOTAL
	Leader	**Contributors**	**Team**	
Vision *Clarity*	1 2 3 4 5 *Dream It*	1 2 3 4 5 *Declare It*	1 2 3 4 5 *Deliver It*	
Insight *Comprehension*	1 2 3 4 5 *Foresight*	1 2 3 4 5 *Hindsight*	1 2 3 4 5 *Engage-sight*	
Collaboration *Chemistry*	1 2 3 4 5 *Communicate*	1 2 3 4 5 *Cooperate*	1 2 3 4 5 *Interact*	
Trust *Confidence*	1 2 3 4 5 *Be Credible*	1 2 3 4 5 *Be Dependable*	1 2 3 4 5 *Be Serving*	
Ownership *Connection*	1 2 3 4 5 *Define*	1 2 3 4 5 *Empower*	1 2 3 4 5 *Implement*	
Resilience *Courage*	1 2 3 4 5 *Acknowledge*	1 2 3 4 5 *Persevere*	1 2 3 4 5 *Overcome*	
Yes *Commitment*	1 2 3 4 5 *Invitation*	1 2 3 4 5 *Alignment*	1 2 3 4 5 *Belief*	
TOTAL				

On a scale of 1–5, with 1 being the lowest, and 5 being the highest, rate how leadership, contributors and the overall team (actors) are doing for each factor element.

Take a moment to tally your score for each row and column. The sum value for each row should range somewhere between 3 and 15, whereas the sum value for each column should range somewhere between 7 and 35. The scoring guide below is intended to help you determine what these values mean.

Table 7 – The TSL Scorecard Scoring Guide

	Factor Ratings (Row Total)	Actor Ratings (Column Total)
High	11-15	26-35
Medium	7-10	16-25
Low	3-6	7-15

Measuring Your Factors

There are seven factors. Rows that score "High," ranging between 11–15, indicate factors that are core strengths for the overall team. Congratulations. Rows that score between 7–10 indicates factors that are neither bad nor good. And for those between 3-6, that indicates factors that need a bit of work.

Take a moment to identify the top 3 factors for your team. Are they all *high*? If so, you are among the elite, and on a path towards *breaking average*. The question though, is what can you do to leverage your factors of strength going forward? This is important. Also consider asking what can you do to improve on these? Every leader, contributor, and team can get better.

Conversely, identify the bottom 3 factors that you need to work on. Are they all *low*? What can you do to improve them? Every team has factors they can improve. Which specific actor is lowest for these factors? Is it the leader, the contributor, or the overall team that is causing that factor to be low? Take steps to improve upon that by evaluating the associated elements.

Improving The Actors

Each element associated with a factor contributes to the performance of an actor: the leader, the contributors, and the overall team. An actor, which can be made up of one or more entities, is a participant in an action or process. If you have a column marked as *high* that indicates consistent strong performance by an actor.

Take a moment to identify the actor who is the single highest performer. Is it the leader, the contributors, or the team as a whole? Rarely does a team performance exceed the score for a leader or the contributors. John Maxwell calls this the "Law of the Lid." To raise team performance, first raise the "lid" of the leader, then work to raise the "lid" of the contributors. When there is a hunger for personal growth, the overall team performance will rise accordingly.

Conversely, identify the single bottom performer that needs improvement. What factors were lowest for that actor? What can be done to improve upon those low scores? When you raise a low factor by focusing on the weak element, you improve the performance.

BREAKING AVERAGE

Appendix C - The TSL Workbook

Chapter 10 shared key questions to help you assess *team strong leadership* for each of the factors supported by the TSL Scorecard in Appendix B. We have also created a companion workbook identified as *The Breaking Average Field Guide* to help you and your team evaluate each factor and identify what can be done to improve. The companion guide also includes bonus tips.

While the workbook is made available separately as a tool for you and your team, we also provide the evaluation components of the workbook in the context of this appendix to ensure completeness. The separate workbook, however, may be preferred as a companion as it offers more space for capturing notes.

Before you use the evaluation components, be sure to take time to go through the TSL Scorecard and keep it handy. Also, for best results, we recommend reaching out to a certified *Breaking Average* coach, who can guide you and your team. A list of *Breaking Average* coaches is available at www.breaking-average.com.

The workbook examines each factor of the VICTORY Mindset.

- The VISION Factor
- The INSIGHT Factor
- The COLLABORATION Factor
- The TRUST Factor
- The OWNERSHIP Factor
- The RESILIENCE Factor
- The YES Factor

The VISION Factor

The first factor is **vision**. For vision you are evaluating clarity. Clarity is what gives leadership, contributors and the team focus.

1. How is leadership daring to *dream*?

Do you have a dream? A dream represents a vision, and it's the moral obligation of the leader to share the dream. Think of Walt Disney, Harriet Tubman, or John F. Kennedy. These historical figures all had a dream they felt compelled to share. As a result, they succeeded at *breaking average*.

Your TSL score reflects how leadership is daring to dream. Consider how well you think the team knows and understands the vision. Do they have clarity on what the dream is? How is leadership communicating the dream? Write your answers below.

_____

_____

_____

Next, what can be done to improve upon sharing the dream? Are there better ways to communicate it? Know that it's seldom wrong to over communicate a vision. Also consider what is being done to reevaluate the vision on a regular basis. Is the vision fresh, relevant, and focused on *breaking average*?

_____

_____

_____

2. What are the team members doing to *declare* the dream?

Dreaming isn't enough on its own. As a leader, you need others to declare the dream with you. This, incidentally, ties in closely with the Ownership Factor. You want team members to own the dream. That's how they become *team strong contributors*.

Your TSL score reflects how team members are embracing the vision. Are there others on the team who are willing to declare the vision and contribute to it as if it's their own? How have they adopted the dream?

Next, what can you and your team do to improve upon the declaration? A declaration measures the clarity of a team's intent.

---

3. What is the team doing to *deliver* the dream?

The success of a team achieving a vision is not dependent upon the dream or the declaration, it's dependent upon the team delivering it.

Your TSL score reflects how the team has performed in delivering the dream. Consider how they have gotten closer to hitting the vision. Think about how team members are contributing to the cause of *breaking average*.

―――――――――――――――――――――――――――――――――
―――――――――――――――――――――――――――――――――
―――――――――――――――――――――――――――――――――
―――――――――――――――――――――――――――――――――

Next, what can you and your team do to improve upon the delivery? What can be done to exceed expectations? Recognize that it doesn't require a herculean effort. You and your team just need a little progress every day. Progress is how teams meet the vision.

―――――――――――――――――――――――――――――――――
―――――――――――――――――――――――――――――――――
―――――――――――――――――――――――――――――――――
―――――――――――――――――――――――――――――――――

For more tips and suggestions to improve a team's Vision Factor, and experience greater clarity, review the Coaching Insights in Chapter 3, by Barbara Gustavson.

The INSIGHT Factor

The second factor is **insight**. For insight you are evaluating comprehension. Comprehension reflects the degree of understanding by the leader, contributors, and team. It's important to understand how to be proactive in sourcing wisdom and gathering intel. The right questions help lead to better insight.

1. How is leadership seeking *foresight?*

One of the ways insight is accomplished is by using foresight. Foresight is about having intuition. It's about leveraging what you know and what you "sense" to guide your decisions.

Your TSL score reflects how well you are doing to pull in foresight. Consider how you are using your experience, your knowledge, and your strengths. What are you doing to leverage your "Spidey sense" that knows when danger is ahead, or something is off or amiss?

Next, what can you do as a leader to improve upon your foresight? How can you sharpen your axe and "Spidey sense" even more? Do you know your strengths? What are they? What can you do to improve upon them?

2. What are team members doing to share *hindsight*?

Hindsight is the understanding of a situation or event after it has happened or developed. It's about learning from our past, so we can make better decisions in the future. Hindsight is the catalyst for preparation for the next situation.

Your TSL score reflects how well team members are able to share their hindsight. Consider what you are doing as a leader to gather hindsight from them, and how feedback is serving the team?

Next, what can be done to better the hindsight? What can you do to improve feedback, reflection, and retrospectives?

3. What is the team doing to offer *engage-sight*?

They say luck is when preparation meets opportunity. If that's true, then all the preparation in the world gained from foresight and hindsight isn't any good unless you also perform engage-sight. Engage-sight is about the team identifying opportunities; it's characterized by two engage-sight principles from Steven Covey.

1. Be proactive in connecting with others
2. Seek to understand before being understood

Your TSL score reflects how the team is doing in the area of engage-sight. Consider how opportunities are heard and captured. Is the team exhibiting the two engage-sight principles?

Next, what can you and your team do to improve upon their engage-sight? Recognize that when you employ engage-sight, you are positioning a team to *break average*.

For more tips and suggestions to improve a team's Insight, Factor and have greater overall comprehension, review the Coaching Insights in Chapter 4, by Richard Mobley.

The COLLABORATION Factor

The third factor is **collaboration**. For collaboration, you evaluate team chemistry and what you can do to improve it.

1. How is leadership working to *communicate*?

Collaboration begins with leadership being proactive to communicate. Communication is the foundation of collaboration.

Your TSL score reflects how well leadership is doing to communicate with the team. Be honest. If you are the leader, are you hoping collaboration will just happen, or are you proactive in making it happen?

_____

_____

_____

Next, identify what you can do as a leader to improve upon your communication? How can you be a catalyst for creating better team chemistry?

_____

_____

_____

Think about how the two principles for engage-sight mentioned earlier can be used to create meaningful collisions. Remember also that active listening is a crucial part of communication. What can you do to be a more active listener?

2. What are the team members doing to *co-operate*?

Co-operation reflects an environment where team members are working alongside each other in the pursuit of achieving something meaningful.

Your TSL score reflects how you and your team members are doing to co-operate. Consider what *team strong contributors* you have and what they are doing to collaborate.

Next, what can you and your team do to improve upon the level of co-operation? Are there meetings that need to be scrapped? Might there be an Integrated Product Team (IPT) that needs to be established? What objectives and initiatives need to be identified?

3. What is the team doing to *interact*?

Keep in mind, collaboration is a necessary factor to *breaking average*. One element to measure team chemistry is how they interact. Take a moment to examine all the evidence you have in front of you to know how the team is interacting.

Your TSL score reflects how the team is doing to interact. Consider how they are collaborating with each other and with leadership. Is there a strong culture of interaction that's present? How so?

Finally, what can you and your team do to improve upon the interaction? Explore ways to increase collaboration. It will help you with the next factor.

For more tips and suggestions to improve a team's Collaboration and gain greater chemistry, review the Coaching Insights in Chapter 5, by Gloria Burgess.

The TRUST Factor

The fourth factor is **trust**. For trust, you evaluate confidence among the leadership, contributors, and the team, as well as what you can do to improve it.

1. How is leadership staying *credible*?

Trust starts with the leader being credible — credible in the values, credible in the message, and credible in the vision. It's about the law of the picture. To be trusted and believable, you must prove to be trustworthy and dependable.

Your TSL score reflects how well you are doing to be credible as a leader. Consider what you are doing to establish trust with the team. Are you authentic? Are you real? Are you responsive?

_____

_____

_____

Next, what can you do to improve upon your credibility? How can you be a catalyst for creating better team chemistry? What things can you do to show yourself to be even more credible?

_____

_____

_____

2. What are the team members doing to be *dependable*?

Trust is a two-sided coin. Not only do you as a leader need to be credible, but your contributors need to be dependable too. Dependability among team members is the path to team trust.

Your TSL score reflects how team members are being dependable. Consider what team members are doing and not doing. What are the trust issues? In what ways are they falling short?

Next, what can you and your team do to improve upon their level of dependability? Is there a performance improvement plan (PIP) that can be put into place as a means to help guide contributors that are not fulfilling their responsibilities? What boundaries do you need to set as a leader to increase the Trust Factor?

---

3. What is the team doing to *serve*?

The third element of trust is service. When a team is focused on service, the Trust Factor jacks up. We have a tagline in my business that reminds our team of this value. The statement is simply, *"Your Success is our Honor."* For me, when I am reminded of this tagline, it begs the question, *"What am I doing in the service of others that creates success for them?"*

Your TSL score reflects how the team is doing to create trust through service. Consider who your team serves and why. What is the team doing to create success for whom they serve?

Next, identify what you and your team can do to improve upon your service. There's nothing more powerful in *breaking average* than creating trust through service.

For more tips and suggestions to improve the team's Trust Factor and increase the confidence, review the Coaching Insights in Chapter 6, by Jay Johnson.

The OWNERSHIP Factor

The fifth factor is **ownership**. For ownership you evaluate connection and what you can do to improve it. Connection gives individuals on the team a sense of belonging.

1. How is leadership *defining* opportunities?

Leadership should be defining opportunities for connection by creating a cause or a mission that the team can own; both individuals and groups of people.

Your TSL score reflects how well you are doing as a leader to define ownership for others. Consider your team's cause or mission. Do people know what they are connecting to? Is it centered on the principle of *breaking average*? Are you clear on the roles and responsibilities? How are you mapping their values and strengths with your vision?

_____

_____

_____

Next, what can you do to improve upon defining ownership opportunities? How can you create better team buy-in and clearer roles and responsibilities? What can you do to offer something to the people on the team that they can connect to and own?

_____

_____

_____

2. What are the team members *empowered* to do?

Empowerment for team members creates encouragement and engagement. It's a vital element for connecting.

Your TSL score reflects how team members are empowered. Consider how they are offered possession and a voice into the team regarding living out the mission of *breaking average*. What are they empowered to do — or not do?

_____

_____

_____

Next, what can you and your team do to improve upon the level of empowerment? Is there something or someone you are neglecting that can help "own" a responsibility? How can you make the team better with empowerment?

_____

_____

_____

3. What is the team doing to *implement* ideas?

It's important to allow the team — including your fan base — to be able to implement ideas and creatively represent the team. This can be a differentiating element for any team or brand.

Your TSL score reflects how the team has been implementing ideas and creatively representing the team. Consider how you, as a leader, are allowing others to represent and support the team's mission and vision. How are team members embracing ideas and celebrating their ideas that have been implemented?

_____

_____

_____

_____

Finally, what can be done to improve upon the ability for the team to implement ideas, express their creativity, and better execute the mission?

_____

_____

_____

_____

For more tips and suggestions to improve a team's Ownership Factor and experience greater connections, review the Coaching Insights in Chapter 7, by Mike Harbour.

The RESILIENCE Factor

The sixth factor is **resilience**. For resilience, you evaluate the courage of the team and what you can do to improve it. Courage is what grants permission to the leadership, contributors and team to advance despite the fear, doubt, or challenge. Resilience is an important component of *team strong leadership*.

1. How is leadership *acknowledging* the threats?

The first element to being resilient is to acknowledge the challenges and fears that the team faces. When we acknowledge the challenges, we can embrace the opportunity to be courageous.

Your TSL score reflects how well you are acknowledging the threats in front of you. Consider how you, as a leader, are taking initiative to be aware of the challenges, fears, and problems. How might you be turning a blind eye to the opportunities for courage? What are you doing to prepare the team to be resilient?

_____

_____

_____

_____

Next, what can you and your team do to improve the acknowledgment? Remember when you acknowledge the threats and opportunities, you can better learn to activate courage. Courage is what it takes to be resilient.

_____

_____

_____

_____

2. What are team members' level of *perseverance*?

Acknowledging your challenges and fear isn't enough, you need to also persevere.

Your TSL score rates the strength of the overall team members' level of perseverance. Consider how they are preserving. Do they tend to give up, or are they staying focused and resolute?

_____

_____

_____

_____

Next, what can you and your team do to improve upon perseverance? Perseverance is one of the most critical steps of leadership. If your team is not seeing it from you, then you may not see it from them.

_____

_____

_____

_____

3. What is the team doing to show they are *overcomers*?

The third element of resilience is about **overcoming**. Overcoming reflects how the team has learned to improvise and adapt.

Your TSL score reflects what you believe the team has exhibited as overcomers. Consider the attitude you have observed in how they have faced and overcome a challenge or crisis. How does the team support each other and fight through adversity?

_____

_____

_____

Next, what can you and your team do to improve as overcomers? Remember, overcoming is about having hope in the midst of the mess. It's about not giving up. What can you do to encourage your team to fight for the finish in the pursuit of *breaking average*?

_____

_____

_____

For more tips and suggestions to improve a team's Resilience Factor, and increase the courage, review the Coaching Insights in Chapter 8, by Dave Cornell.

The YES Factor

The seventh factor is **yes**. For the Yes Factor you are evaluating commitment and what you can do to improve it. Commitment reflects the "all-in" mentality of the leaders, contributors and team. It is critical to *breaking average*.

1. How is leadership offering the *invite*?

Commitment begins with leadership being proactive in creating an invitation. We need others to feel invited to join our cause.

Your TSL score reflects how well leadership is doing to offer the invitation. How is leadership offering the invite? If you are a leader, consider what you are doing to invite others to join you on the journey. Write your answers below

---

Remember, new leaders lead because they feel a sense of invitation. They feel called. Great leaders extend the calling by inviting others to join the cause. Ask yourself what can you do to improve upon the invitation? What are some proactive steps you can take?

---

2. What are team members doing to *align* with the plan?

It's important that team members are aligned with the mission and vision. Without proper alignment of *team strong contributors*, there can be dysfunctionality. Instead of a team of contributors all rowing in sync for a great cause, you get busyness without great impact

Your TSL score reflects how the team members are doing in the area of alignment. Consider how contributors on your team are aligned with your mission and vision. How do they see their values reflected in the vision?

_____

_____

_____

Next, what can you and your team do to improve upon the alignment? This is super ultra-important. If the team is not aligning with the vision then it's going to be a struggle – and, at best, you will have to settle for average. However, if you want your team to *break average*, then work to create alignment.

_____

_____

_____

3. What is the team doing to show they *believe* in the cause?

The third element to the Yes Factor is believe. Attitude is a key lever to overcoming challenges. All-time great football coach Lou Holtz, once remarked, *"Virtually nothing is impossible in this world if you just put your mind to it and maintain a positive attitude."* Belief is the most powerful attitude of them all.

Your TSL score reflects how the team is doing to show they believe in both the cause, and in the leadership. Consider the evidence and signs that show they believe. Think about their attitude and story. Is it one that causes others to believe too?

_____

_____

_____

Next, what can you and your team do to improve upon the belief? Are there ways that you as a leader can inject greater belief? How can attitude influence the team?

_____

_____

_____

For more tips and suggestions to improve a team's Yes Factor, and achieve the commitment you need, review the Coaching Insights in Chapter 9, by Trudy Menke.

Appendix D - Additional Resources

There are some great resources on teamwork that go even deeper for each of these factors. Here are a few of our favorites that we recommend.

Teamwork Resources

- Mark Miller, *"The Secret of Teams"*, October 2011.

- John C. Maxwell, *"The 17 Indisputable Laws of Teamwork: Embrace Them and Empower Your Team"*, July 2001.

- Patrick Lencioni, *"The Five Dysfunctions of a Team: A Leadership Fable"*, April 2002.

- Jim Collins, *"Good to Great: Why Some Companies Make the Leap... And Others Don't"*, October 2001.

Vision Factor Resources

- John C. Maxwell, *"Put Your Dream to the Test: 10 Question to Help You See It and Seize It"*, March 2009.

- Simon Sinek, *"The Infinite Game"*, October 2019.

- Barbara Valentine Gustavson, *"Permission to be Bold: A Guide to Loving Yourself, Living Fully, and Leaving Your Mark in the World"*, Lead Edge Press, December 2018.

- Daniel Floyd, *"Living the Dream: Uncover the Plan. Fulfill Your Purpose"*, April 2013

- Mark Batterson, *"The Circle Maker: Praying Circles Around Your Biggest Dreams and Greatest Fears"*, Expanded Edition, December 2016.

- Chris McCheney, Sean Covey, Jim Huling, *"The 4 Disciplines of Execution: Achieving Your Wildly Important Goals"*, April 2012.

Insight Factor Resources

- Simon Sinek, *"Start with Why: How Great Leaders Inspire Everyone to Take Action"*, October 2009.

- Ray Dalio, *"Principles: Life and Work"*, September 2017.

- John C. Maxwell, *"How Successful People Think"*, June 2009.

- Napoleon Hill, *"Think and Grow Rich"*, 1937.

- Daniel Kahneman, *"Thinking, Fast and Slow"*, October 2011.

Collaboration Factor Resources

- Daniel Coyle, *"The Culture Code: The Secrets of Highly Successful Groups"*, January 2018.

- John C. Maxwell, *"Everyone Communicates, Few Connect: What the Most Effective People Do Differently"*, March 2010.

- Ed Catmull, *"Creativity, Inc: Overcoming the Unseen Forces that Stan in the Way of True Inspiration"*, April 2014.

- Andy Stanley, *"Creating Community: Five Key to Building a Small Group Culture"*, December 2004.

Trust Factor Resources

- David Horsager, *"The Trust Edge: How Top Leaders Gain Faster Results, Deeper Relationships, and a Stronger Bottom Line"*, October 2012.

- John G. Miller, *"QBQ! The Question Behind the Question: Practicing Personal Accountability at Work and in Life"*, September 2004.

- Stephen M.R. Covey, *"The Speed of Trust: The One Thing That Changes Everything"*, February 2008.

- Chris Brogan and Julien Smith, *"Trust Agents: Using the Web to Build Influence, Improve Reputation, and Earn Trust"*, August 2009.

Ownership Factor Resources

- Captain D. Michael Abrashoff, *"It's Your Ship: Management Techniques from the Best Damn Ship in the Navy"*, 10th Anniversary Edition, October 2012.

- Jocko Willink, Leif Babin, *"Extreme Ownership: How U.S. Navy SEALS Lead and Win"*, Nov 2017.

- John C. Maxwell, *"Leadershift: The 11 Essential Changes Every Leader Must Embrace"*, Feb 2019.

- Dr. Henry Cloud, *"Boundaries for Leaders: Results, Relationships, and Being Ridiculously in Charge"*, April 2013.

Resilience Resources

- Bonnie St. John, *"Micro-Resilience: Minor Shift for Major Boosts in Focus, Drive, and Energy"*, February 2017.

- Dave Cornell, *"Cultivating Courage: Face Fear, Fulfill Dreams"*, November 2018.

- Paul Gustavson, *"Leader Press On: Discovering the Power of Perseverance"*, Lead Edge Press, May 2016.

- Angela Duckworth, *"Grit: The Power of Passion and Perseverance"*, May 2016.

Yes Factor Resources

- Barry Smith, *"Leadership by Invitation: How to RSVP and Embrace Your Role as a LEADER"*, May 2014.

- Kerry Petersen, *"Crucial Accountability: Tools for Resolving Violated Expectations, Broken Commitment, and Bad Behavior"*, August 2004.

- Patrick Lencioni, *"The Ideal Team Player: How to Recognize and Cultivate the Three Essential Virtues"*, April 2016.

- John Maxwell, *"Good Leaders Ask Great Questions: Your Foundation for Successful Leadership"*, October 2017.

Appendix E - Power Quotes

Throughout the book, we have used multiple quotes to emphasize and make points. There are additional quotes that we didn't necessarily leverage in the text that we wanted to offer here as well to encourage you with teamwork as it pertains to each of the *team strong leadership* factors. Enjoy!

Teamwork Quotes

- "It is amazing what you can accomplish if you do not care who gets the credit." – Harry S Truman

- "We rise by lifting others" – Robert Ingersoll

- "Find a group of people who challenge and inspire you, spend a lot of time with them, and it will change your life forever." – Amy Poehler

- "Teamwork is a strategic decision." – Patrick Lencioni

- "The strength of the team is each individual member. The strength of each member is the team." – Phil Jackson

- "There is no such thing as a self-made man. You will reach your goals only with the help of others." – George Shinn

Vision Factor Quotes

- "Vision is the art of seeing what is invisible to others." – Johnathan Swift

- "Have a vision. It is the ability to see the invisible. If you can see the invisible, you can achieve the impossible." – Shiv Khera

- "All our dreams can come true if we have the courage to pursue them." – Walt Disney

- "Make your vision so clear that your fears become irrelevant." – Anonymous

- "Do not go where the path may lead, go instead where there is no path and leave a trail." – Ralph Waldo Emerson

Insight Factor Quotes

- "Speed is often confused with insight. When I start running earlier than the others, I appear faster." – Johan Cruyff

- "Do not discount ideas from unexpected sources. Inspiration can, and does, come from anywhere." – Ed Catmull

- "With an open mind, we gain insight into ideas and expressions that we may have overlooked or not noticed at all." – James Van Praagh

Collaboration Factor Quotes

- "Great things in business are never done by one person. They're done by a team of people" – Steve Jobs

- "A company's communication structure should not mirror its organizational structure. Everybody should be able to talk to anybody." – Ed Catmull

- "There are two ways of exerting one's strength: one is pushing down, the other is pulling up." – Booker T. Washington

- "None of us is as smart as all of us." – Ken Blanchard

Trust Factor Quotes

- "Trust not money is the currency of business and life. In a climate of Trust, people are more creative, motivated, productive and willing to sacrifice for the team." – David Horsager

- "The moment there is suspicion about a person's motives, everything he does becomes tainted." – Mahatma Gandhi

- "The glue that holds all relationships together — including the relationship between the leader and the led — is trust, and trust is based on integrity." – Brian Tracy

- "He who does not trust enough will not be trusted." – Lao Tzu

Ownership Factor Quotes

- "Responsibility equals accountability equals ownership. And a sense of ownership is the most powerful weapon a team or organization can have. – Pat Summit

- "Leaders must own everything in their world. There is no one else to blame." – Jocko Willink

- "Something happens when you feel ownership. You no longer act like a spectator or consumer, because you're an owner." – Bob Goff

- "Finding and fixing problems is everybody's job. Anyone should be able to stop the production line." – Ed Catmull

Resilience Quotes

- "The greatest glory in living lies not in never falling, but in rising every time we fall." – Ralph Waldo Emerson

- "Only those who dare to fail greatly can ever achieve greatly." – Robert F. Kennedy

- "If you're going through hell, keep going." – Winston Churchill

- "Courage doesn't always roar. Sometimes courage is the quiet voice at the end of the day saying, 'I will try again tomorrow'." – Mary Ann Radmacher

Yes Factor Quotes

- "Teamwork requires some sacrifice up front; people who work as a team have to put the collective needs of the group ahead of their individual interests." – Patrick Lencioni

- "When you're surrounded by people who share a passionate commitment around a common purpose, anything is possible." – Howard Schultz

- "There is no abiding success without commitment." – Tony Robbins

- "The attitude of giving a full commitment to the partnership will usually result in getting the same commitment in return." – Denise Morrison

VICTORY Quotes

- "Leaders find a way for the team to win." – John C. Maxwell

- "Victory is always possible for the person who refuses to stop fighting." – Napoleon Hill

- "If you believe in yourself and have dedication and pride - and never quit, you'll be a winner. The price of victory is high but so are the rewards." – Bear Bryant

- "In reading the lives of great men, I found that the first victory they won was over themselves... self-discipline with all of them came first." – Harry S. Truman

Acknowledgements

I want to thank my contributing authors who have helped shape this book. Each of them is an amazing leader and they are all passionate about adding value to others. I could spend all day highlighting their virtues and impact that they have made in my life. I truly value and honor the impact they have made in the lives of others. If you are in need of a coach or a speaker centered on the topic of teamwork or any of these seven factors, take time to reach out to one of them. As I have personally experienced, they are all equipped to help guide and serve you. They care deeply for those that they serve.

I want to thank the review team and mentors who also helped shape this project. Specifically, Jeff Grogan, Tiffany Johnson , and James Spann. Your contributions and candor in the final stages were truly impactful. I also want to thank Karen Anderson, who early on encouraged me to push forward on this project.

I want to thank Team SimVentions. It's hard to believe we've been doing this for 20 years. The continuous improvement we have been pursuing gives me hope that the next 20+ years will be even better. I value each of you. I especially want to thank Joe Caliri for helping shape a renewed perspective for me and my fellow co-founders on what it takes to be *team strong leaders*. I truly feel blessed and believe that the best is yet to come.

As a person of faith, I want to thank God for the provisions, wisdom, and blessings. Faith for me is a critical component to all of this. If you want to amplify any of the seven critical factors that we've discussed, then lean in on your faith. If you lack wisdom, ask. If you need hope, seek. If you want opportunities, knock. His promise is that the door will be opened to you. What's in front of us is an egress to *breaking average,* and a means to bless others. That's what we are called to do.

Finally, I want to thank my family for their support, and encouragement. Barb, Ryan, Michael and Wani, you are the greatest team of all!

Yours in Leadership,

Paul Gustavson

P.S. Now go break average!

Notes

Introduction

[1]   John Donne, *"No Man is an Island"*,
       https://web.cs.dal.ca/~johnston/poetry/island.html, last accessed on
       March 22, 2020.

[2]   Gretchen Schmidt, *"Small Business Statistics: 19 Essential
       Numbers You Need to Know"*, updated January 8, 2020,
       https://www.fundera.com/blog/small-business-statistics, last
       accessed on January 11, 2020.

[3]   Simon Sinek. *"The Infinite Game"*, (pp. 32-33). Penguin
       Publishing.

Chapter 1

[4]   *"Al Ulbrickson, University of Washington crew,"* Seattle, 1937,
       https://digitalcollections.lib.washington.edu/digital/collection/imls
       mohai/id/938/, last accessed on January 11, 2020.

[5]   *"Husky Crew, Chronicles Coach Al Ulbrickson's career"*,
       http://www.huskycrew.com/1930.htm, last accessed on Jan 11,
       2020.

[6]   Dr. Henry Murray, Harvard Psychological Clinic, *"The Analysis
       and Personality of Adolph Hitler: With Predictions of His Future
       Behavior and Suggestions for Dealing With Him Now and After
       Germany's Surrender"*, written October, 1943,
       https://www.cia.gov/library/readingroom/docs/CIA-RDP78-
       02646R000100030002-2.pdf, last accessed on March 7, 2020.

[7]   Michael Socolow, *"Six Minutes in Berlin"*, written July 23, 2012
       http://www.slate.com/articles/sports/fivering_circus/2012/07/_193
       6_olympics_rowing_the_greatest_underdog_nazi_defeating_ameri
       can_olympic_victory_you_ve_never_heard_of_.html, last accessed
       on January 11, 2020.

[8]   *"The Rowing Team that Stunned the World"*, written July 04,
        2013, https://www.wbur.org/hereandnow/2013/07/04/berlin-
        olympics-rowing, last accessed on January 11, 2020.

[8]   Author's Note: There was much more to the 1936 Olympic story
        that we did not touch on. We have done our best to accurately
        reflect the historical account, but to fill some of the gaps in the
        story, a few creative liberties were made to help portray the story
        and make it feel as if you were there.

        We highly encourage you to read *"Boys in The Boat"* by Daniel
        James Brown to learn more about this incredible team and their
        extraordinary accomplishment. His story goes deeper in unpacking
        the impact of the era: The Great Depression and the struggles of
        young men trying to survive, the Olympic world stage that Hitler
        used to promote his power, and so much more.

        Reports are that George Clooney will be turning *"Boys in The
        Boat"* into a full production movie. I wonder if Clooney will cast
        himself in the role of Ulbrickson. He'd be a good one.

Chapter 2

[10]   Mike Kappel, *"6 Ways to Measure Small Business Success"*,
        written March 8, 2017,
        https://www.forbes.com/sites/mikekappel/2017/03/08/6-ways-to-
        measure-small-business-success/#136c0a7118f4, last accessed on
        January 11, 2020.

[11]   David McCullough, *"The Wright Brothers"*, Simon & Schuster;
        First Edition, May 5, 2015.

[12]   Walt Disney, https://en.wikipedia.org/wiki/Walt_Disney, last
        accessed on January 11, 2020.

[13]   *Snow White and the Seven Dwarfs* (1937 film),
        https://en.wikipedia.org/wiki/Snow_White_and_the_Seven_Dwarf
        s_(1937_film), last accessed on January 11, 2020.

[14]   Movie, *"42: The True Story of an American Legend"*, Warner Bros, 12 April 2013.

[15]   Samantha DiFeliciantonio, *"The Importance of Teamwork"*, November 18, 2016, https://www.teambonding.com/teamwork-is-important/, last accessed on January 11, 2020.

Chapter 3

[16]   Tony Dungy, *"Quiet Strength: The Principles, Practices, and Priorities of a Winning Life"*, Tyndale Momentum, June 1, 2008

[17]   Paul Gustavson, *"The Birth of a Nation Started with a Question"*, written July 2, 2016, http://paulgustavson.net/the-birth-of-a-nation/, last accessed on January 11, 2020.

[18]   Bill Taylor, *"What Breaking the 4-Minute Mile Taught Us About the Limits of Conventional Thinking"*, written March 9, 2018, https://hbr.org/2018/03/what-breaking-the-4-minute-mile-taught-us-about-the-limits-of-conventional-thinking, last accessed on January 11, 2020.

[19]   Mike Wall, *"Apollo 11: Why JFK Believed His Bold Moonshot Could Actually Happen"*, written July 17, 2019, https://www.space.com/jfk-apollo-moonshot-nasa-readiness.html, last accessed on January 11, 2020.

Chapter 4

[20]   Movie, *"Hidden Figures"*, Fox Pictures, 2016.

[21]   Walter Isaacson, *"The Innovators: How a Group of Hackers, Geniuses, and Geeks Created the Digital Revolution"*, Simon & Schuster, October 6, 2015.

[22]   Howard Schultz, *"Onward: How Starbucks Fought for Its Life without Losing Its Soul"*, March 27, 2012.

[23]   Author Stephen Covey identified these two principles in his classic book *The 7 Habits of Highly Effective People*

[24]   The Message, Proverbs 20:5

[25]   Mark Batterson, *"Primal: A Quest for the Lost Soul of Christianity"*, Multnomah Books, December 22, 2009."

[26]   Ed Catmull, *"Creativity, Inc.: Overcoming the Unseen Forces That Stand in the Way of True Inspiration"*, Random House, April 8, 2014

Chapter 5

[27]   Don Daszkowskim *"The Story of S. Truett Cathy, From One Tiny Restaurant to a $1.6-Billion Chick-fil-A Empire"*, https://www.thebalancesmb.com/s-truett-cathy-bio-chick-fil-a-story-1350972, last accessed on January 11, 2020.

[28]   Live event with Dan Cathy, "John Maxwell Team, 2014 International Maxwell Certification, Orlando, Florida

[29]   *Chick-fil-A Values*, https://www.comparably.com/companies/chick-fil-a/mission, last accessed on January 11, 2020.

[30]   Daniel Coyle, *"The Culture Code: The Secret of Highly Successful Groups"*, Bantam Books.

[31]   Merriam Webster Dictionary Online, "comradery", https://www.merriam-webster.com/dictionary/comradery, last accessed on January 11, 2020.

[32]   *The MoSCoW method*, https://en.wikipedia.org/wiki/MoSCoW_method, last accessed on January 11, 2020.

Chapter 6

[33]   Movie, *"12 Strong"*, Warner Brothers, 2018.

[34]   Movie, *"Braveheart"*, Warner Brothers, 1995.

[35] Brené Brown, *"Dare to Lead: Brave Work. Tough Conversations. Whole Hearts."*, Random house, October 2018.

[36] David Horsager, *"The Trust Edge: How Top Leaders Gain Faster Results, Deeper Relationships, and a Stronger Bottom Line"*, Free Press, October 2012.

Chapter 7

[37] Andy Grove, *"Only the Paranoid Survive: How to Exploit the Crisis Points That Challenge Every Company"*, Random House, Mar 16, 1999.

[38] Intel Website, *"Intel at 50: The 8086 and Operation Crush"* https://newsroom.intel.com/news/intel-50-8086-operation-crush/#gs.rban3t, last accessed on January 11, 2020.

[39] John Doerr, *"Measure What Matters: How Google, Bono, and the Gates Foundation Rock the World with OKRs"*, Portfolio, April 24, 2018

[40] Korn Ferry Institute, *"Alan Mulally: The Man Who Saved Ford"*, https://www.kornferry.com/institute/alan-mulally-man-who-saved-ford, last accessed on January 11, 2020.

Chapter 8

[41] Movie, *"Apollo 13"*, Universal Pictures, 1995.

[42] Brené Brown, *"Rising Strong: How the Ability to Reset Transforms the Way We Live, Love, Parent, and Lead"*, Random House, Aug 2015.

Chapter 9

[43] Movie, *"The Greatest Showman"*, 20th Century Fox, 2017.

[44] Brent Lang, *"Hugh Jackman on 'The Greatest Showman,'*, https://variety.com/2017/film/features/hugh-jackman-the-greatest-showman-logan-1202629864/, last accessed on January 11, 2020.

[45] *"The Greatest Showman | Behind the Scenes"*, 20th Century FOX, https://www.youtube.com/watch?v=aLT0EAR6amk

[46] Hippo Valley Christian Mission, Zimbabwe, www.hippovalley.org, last accessed on January 11, 2020.

Chapter 10

[47] Simon Sinek, *"The Infinite Game"*, Penguin Publishing Group.

[48] The King James Bible, Proverbs 16:18.

[49] Simon Sinek, *"The Infinite Game"*, Penguin Publishing Group.

[50] This quote and thought is attributed to John C. Maxwell.

[51] Donald Miller, *"Building a StoryBrand: Clarify Your Message So Customers Will Listen"*, HarperCollins, October 2017.

About the Authors

Paul Gustavson — Principle Author

Paul Gustavson is a cofounder and CTO of *SimVentions, Inc.*, a technology firm supporting today's military with innovative engineering solutions. *SimVentions* has been recognized as one of Virginia's Best Places to Work and was named by *Inc. Magazine* as one of "The 50 Best Places to Work in 2016". As the CTO, Paul leads in identifying and contributing to the company's capability and influencing the strategic vision. Paul is also the author of the books *Leaders Press On* and *Speech Blueprint* and is co-host of the *Transformational Leader Podcast*. He is an active member within the simulation and virtual reality communities. Paul and his wife Barbara live in Virginia.

You can connect with Paul at http://www.simventions.com

Trudy Menke — The Yes Factor

Trudy Menke is the President of *Reframing Leadership, LLC* and a founding member of the *John Maxwell Team*. Her career as an executive coach and team trainer focuses on improving clarity and results through strengthening leadership and communication skills. For more than 25 years, Trudy has built her expertise in leadership within sales, training, marketing and team building. She and her husband, Brian, have been married for over 30 years, raised two daughters and enjoy calling Indiana home.

You can connect with Trudy at https://trudymenke.com.

Dave Cornell — The Resilience Factor

Dave Cornell is the founder and president of *Cultivate Courage, LLC*, an organization dedicated to helping others overcome their fears and lead their most courageous life. Dave is a speaker, coach, and trainer focusing on personal development and leadership. For over 35 years he was in sales, sales management, and training and development. He is the author of *Cultivate Courage*. Dave lives in Fergus Falls, Minnesota with his wife Amy. They have two daughters, one son-in-law and four grandchildren.

You can connect with Dave at http://www.cultivatecourage.com

Mike Harbour — The Ownership Factor

Mike Harbour is the founder and Chief Action Officer for *Harbour Resources*, whose mission is to ignite purpose, excellence and action for leaders and organizations across the United States. Mike serves as chair for the John Maxwell Transformational Leadership Award, and he is a Peer Teaching Partner for over 30,000 fellow coaches, speakers and trainers around the world. Mike lives in Little Rock, Arkansas with his son and daughter and wife of 27 plus years.

You can connect with Mike at http://www.harbourresources.com.

Barbara Gustavson — The Vision Factor

Barbara Gustavson, founder of *Discover Next Step*, equips individuals and teams to embrace their strengths and give themselves permission to step boldly into their potential. Barbara is a certified Personal Development Coach and an *Amen Clinic* Brain Health Coach. By combining leadership concepts with neuroscience and brain health, her clients experience improvements in their business, life and well-being. She is the author of the book *Permission To Be BOLD*. She and her husband live in Virginia and have two older sons and a daughter-in-law.

You can connect with Barbara at http://discovernextstep.com.

Jay Johnson — The Trust Factor

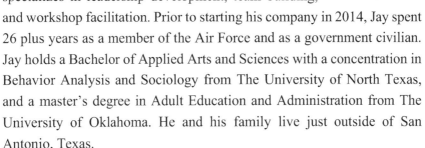

A retired Air Force veteran, Jay Johnson owns and operates *J2 Servant Leadership, LLC*, a training and consulting company. In addition to speaking and training domestically and abroad, Jay is also a certified Change Manager and Coach, who specializes in leadership development, team building, and workshop facilitation. Prior to starting his company in 2014, Jay spent 26 plus years as a member of the Air Force and as a government civilian. Jay holds a Bachelor of Applied Arts and Sciences with a concentration in Behavior Analysis and Sociology from The University of North Texas, and a master's degree in Adult Education and Administration from The University of Oklahoma. He and his family live just outside of San Antonio, Texas.

You can connect with Jay at https://j2servantleadership.com/.

Richard Mobley — The Insight Factor

Richard Mobley is a principal in *The Seven Four Group*, a consulting firm specializing in executive, team and personal leadership development. The firm provides value through knowledge, relationships, background and resources to improve the status quo. During his successful career journey, he has served in executive leadership in the corporate world — primarily in healthcare business operations. Mr. Mobley has had the privilege of beginning businesses from the ground up, including a consulting and coaching business founded in 2006. He has experienced the impact of good leadership, poor leadership and no leadership. These experiences produced an intense passion for excellent leadership.

You can connect with Richard at https://sevenfourgroup.com.

Gloria Burgess, PhD — The Collaboration Factor

Gloria Burgess is founder and CEO of two organizations that equip and inspire leaders throughout the world. A retired executive in IT, philanthropy, and human services, she is a highly sought-after speaker and strategic advisor. Gloria is faculty and founding partner with the John Maxwell Team, and she also serves as faculty in executive leadership at Northwest University, University of Washington, University of Southern California, and Slovenia's IEDC Bled School of Management. Her recent books include *Pass It On!*, featuring her father's divinely-appointed friendship with Nobel laureate William Faulkner, and *Flawless Leadership*.

You can connect with Gloria at http://gloriaburgess.com.

Made in the USA
Columbia, SC
11 June 2020